WINNER INSTINCT

2ND REVISED EDITION

LESLIE BENDALY
AND
NICOLE BENDALY

iUniverse®

WINNER INSTINCT
2ND REVISED EDITION

iUniverse books may be ordered through booksellers or by contacting:

iUniverse
1663 Liberty Drive
Bloomington, IN 47403
www.iuniverse.com
1-800-Authors (1-800-288-4677)

ISBN: 978-1-5320-6595-8 (sc)
ISBN: 978-1-5320-6596-5 (e)

Print information available on the last page.

iUniverse rev. date: 01/21/2019

Contents

Introduction

Success Is Yours for the Taking

Talk about being in the right place at the right time. It's as though we have all won some sort of universal lottery. Of all the times in which we could have been living, here we are in the Age of Possibility. It offers more opportunities than ever before, more possibilities than ever before. We should wake up every morning with all the excitement of a child in a toy store.

Each of us can shape our place in this new world, as difficult as it may sometimes seem. Success today can be unprecedented, whether to you it means fame, fortune, position, prestige, personal fulfillment and accomplishment, or inner peace and happiness. *Winner Instinct* is designed to help you increase the personal power you need in order to achieve—with greater ease—whatever you desire. There is one qualifier: You must be able to believe that success depends not on what *happens* to you, but on how you *respond to what happens* to you.

People are always blaming their circumstances for what they are. I don't believe in circumstances. The people who get on in this world are the people who get up and look for the circumstances they want, and, if they can't find them, make them.

George Bernard Shaw

Increased Change Means Increased Opportunity

The period of transition in which we live and work has been described as the most dramatic in recorded history. Such transitions come along every few hundred years, but none—not even the Industrial Revolution—brought the pace and magnitude of change our world is currently experiencing. The late and highly respected futurist Alvin Toffler put it this way:

> A new civilization is emerging in our lives and blind men everywhere are trying to suppress it. This new civilization brings with it new family styles, changed ways of working, loving, and living, a new economy, new political conflicts, and beyond all this an altered consciousness as well.[11]

Today each of us faces more unknowns than ever before, and they are coming at us at merciless speed. We must be prepared to meet those unknowns. Some people do so with ease, while others struggle. Many eventually fall by the wayside.

Hyper-paced change is quickly sorting people and organizations into two camps: those who succeed with ease and those who struggle to

---

[1] *Alvin and Heidi Toffler. Creating a New Civilization: The Politics of the Third Wave. Atlanta: Turner, 1995.*

keep up. Even people who used to do a "pretty good job" are finding that their best is no longer good enough. New skills must constantly be learned. We must spend more time collaborating and sharing information and decisions with others, which means attending meetings that cut into our already precious time.

Technology, like many aspects of our new reality, is paradoxical in nature—on the one hand, making the job easier; on the other, increasing expectations and workload. There are no more excuses. Immediate action is the expectation. The overload of information requires us to filter the vital information from the nonessential, but sometimes we sacrifice what may be of interest to us along the way.

Technology enables multi-tasking: moms and dads on their cell phones and tablets while at their kids' soccer games, being available for a virtual meeting while on vacation, and pulling out a laptop while watching a movie with your partner on the couch to "quickly" respond to a few dozen emails. Busy-ness and multi-tasking do not equate to performance; the act of always being connected and able to immediately respond creates the *illusion* of performance but mostly creates detachment from the present moment, increased stress and the unending feeling of never quite being able to keep up with both personal and business expectations.

We meet people in our workshops who attend up to thirty meetings a week, sort through more than one hundred e-mails daily, attend training courses and have taken on additional workloads, while trying desperately to attain a measure of work/life balance. Many, not surprisingly, struggle to maintain their performance level not to mention their own mental and physical well-being.

There is no longer an "also placed" category. "Pretty good" performance doesn't count for much anymore. You either win or you don't. If that thought instantly increased your stress level, here's the antidote: *There is room for each of us in the winner's circle and* ***each of us*** *can* get there *without struggle and without having to sacrifice what is of most importance to each of us in life.* (Note: Without struggle does not mean without hard work!)

> *There's no need to stand behind anyone when there's so much room to walk.*
>
> Rene Mickenberg, *Taxi Driver Wisdom*

Getting to the Winner's Circle

So what's the difference between those who succeed with ease and those who struggle to achieve? Sometimes one's laziness, arrogance, narrow-mindedness or negative attitude disqualify them from competing in a work world that demands hard effort, responsiveness and flexibility. But more often than not, the winners and those struggling to keep up have much in common. The "strugglers" often work just as hard as—often harder than—the winners, keep their knowledge and skills up to date and may even have positive attitudes.

What then is THE difference? Those who achieve with greater ease have *winner instinct.*

Winner instinct is new-world street smarts. It is an ability to understand the new and often daunting world of work and business at a gut level. It is the ability to "get it"—to understand the requirements of the new game we are playing. Winner instinct allows us to respond intuitively, quickly and wisely to whatever is around the corner. It gives us the personal power to fulfill our goals and dreams.

For people with winner instinct, life includes many pleasant, but not totally unexpected, surprises. They *know* they are "lucky." But it is their winner instinct that allows them to influence their luck, and that attracts fortunate circumstances to them.

And importantly, they are enthusiastically in tune with the world around them. They could be a success at any time or in any place, because they instinctively understand the laws that are in motion. They understand the importance of something Cecil B. De Mille said: "We cannot break the laws. We can only break ourselves against the laws." The new knowledge-based economy and the new civilization Toffler describes bring with them a set of new laws. If you are not working in concert with these laws, you may as well be throwing balls up in the air and expecting them to stay there. Your efforts will prove futile.

Those with winner instinct recognize that the knowledge-based world we are living and working in is—to use an apropos cliché —a whole new ball game. The rules that determine success have been quietly rewritten. If you are unknowingly playing by the old rules, you will never hit a home run. That's just the way it is.

The 6 New Laws of Success

There are six new requirements that govern the way the new world works. Each is already fully in play and if you intend to succeed with ease you need to recognize and embrace them.

1: Embrace the New Renaissance

Those with winner instinct are New Renaissance people. They know they must be knowledge-based and values-based people. They are able to spot trends early and make use of that information.

2: Walk Fast on Thin Ice

There is no point in waiting for the ice to thicken; thin ice has become a permanent condition. Nothing is for sure. We are all acutely aware that jobs and companies disappear, that a financial sneeze in the Far East can quickly turn into an epidemic of recessions. It takes know-how and personal balance to walk fast on thin ice. Our ability to do this depends on our personal Task/Process balance.

3: Live with Purpose and Passion

As the pace of change continues to accelerate, work stress grows exponentially. Enthusiasm has always given people an edge—today it is a basic requirement. Those who are working at a job they do not enjoy will quickly burn out—or be turned out.

People who excel have found a way to earn a living—and usually a very comfortable one—having fun. These people are doing what they are meant to do, and doing it with passion.

4: Get Interconnected

Being isolated in our highly connected world sucks the value from your knowledge and skills. Your personal power is in direct proportion to the *number* and *quality* of your connections with others. But getting connected doesn't just happen.

5: Tap Your Intuition

Applying logic based on what we learned yesterday to information that was collected yesterday can't prepare us to succeed in an unknown tomorrow. Fortunately, you have a powerful resource and one that few people tap: intuition. Better use of your intuition will not only enable you to spot opportunities and respond to them, but will give you a definite edge over the many who are trying to get by on logic alone.

6: Promote Yourself

High Performance = Personal Success? That equation sounds reasonable and fair, but you know what they say about life and fairness. At one time, you could have done a good job and then sat quietly in your corner, knowing that someone would eventually move you at least a rung or two up the corporate ladder or discover your amazing product or service. You would be *offered* an opportunity. Today, you have to *find* that opportunity and convince others that it is meant to be *your* opportunity. You may very well be the best at what you do, but if you sit quietly, people you need to influence will walk right by you—even if it is an "inferior product" that attracts their attention.

****

If you are, to paraphrase De Mille, "breaking yourself against a law," then you will suffer stress, frustration and, not uncommonly, fatigue and even illness.

Winner Instinct is designed to help you achieve what you are meant to achieve, and to do so greater ease.

Don't just read this book—use it. We are convinced that one of the greatest weaknesses of most of us who strive to be better is not applying what we already know. We busily search for more information, and for new and better solutions and fixes. Once we've found them, instead of using them we continue to search for newer, and therefore—we think—even better answers. It is always easier to gather information than it is to make use of it.

Winner's Tip: To get the most from *Winner Instinct*, as you go through it don't ask yourself "Do I already know this?", but rather "Do I do this?"

At the end of each chapter you will find Workouts for developing winner instinct. If you choose to use them they will provide more in-depth how-to's for getting in flow with each of the laws plus exercises you can use to help you hone the required practices and skills.

As you explore the new requirements, some will immediately make sense, and your response will be "Yes, of course." You may greet other requirements with less enthusiasm. If your reaction to an idea is "That's crazy," or you feel even a nagging discomfort, I encourage you to explore that section thoroughly. Chances are that it describes a required behavior that is not part of your instinctive personal repertoire, and that is therefore of particular importance to you. There is little or no growth in the comfort zone. Discomfort frequently indicates a growth opportunity, and winners grab onto those opportunities and focus on turning them into strengths.

A Personal Perspective

Every book is influenced by the author's values and beliefs, so we think it is only fair that we share those of ours that most relate to *Winner Instinct.*

- We believe that inside each of us is an even better, happier and more successful person trying to get out, that we each have been endowed with a particular ability and that each of us has an important contribution to make. Once we discover this ability and use it in concert with the new laws, we will experience success.

- Our success requires that we concentrate on what we have to contribute, rather than on what we have to gain. This is not as altruistic as it sounds. The greater our contribution, the more we will receive—that is, the greater will be our success. This is why the "what's-in-it-for-me" attitude doesn't work. It goes against the flow of the new world order. Today we must focus on what we're giving. The getting will follow.
- There is a beautiful synchronicity in the world. Once we are tuned in to it, we will succeed with ease.
- Each of us has an opportunity to influence in some way big or small the new civilization that is emerging.
- Those who will make the greatest contribution, and experience the greatest joy, in this exceptional world we live and work in will have *Winner Instinct.*

Law #1

EMBRACE THE NEW RENAISSANCE

If you plan to have the world by the tail, you'd better have a good understanding of the world. A New Renaissance is upon us. The parallels between the early 21st-century and the 15th-century renaissance may not immediately be apparent, but they are meaningful to anyone who plans to develop winner instinct.

The Renaissance was a period of rebirth of culture and education. During the Dark Ages, the appreciation of beauty and pursuit of knowledge had been smothered. As the writings that had been hoarded in secluded monasteries became broadcast and as universities were developed, knowledge became more widely accessible. The "Renaissance man" was not only broadly educated and skilled, but was expected to know himself. This was a time of accelerated transition, and that energy sparked creativity.

In the New Renaissance, access to learning has been exponentially expanded by the Internet. The New Renaissance person must have an eclectic knowledge base in order to function in the interconnected, change-happens-in-a-nanosecond, 21st century.

Become an Environmental Scanner

Ignorance is not bliss. Today, we have to be even better informed than in the past. This does not mean being a Jeopardy champion. Having a head that is chock full of dates, names and places is of benefit only if the information can be used. We must aim not only to be informed, but to be knowledgeable.

Gathering information is the first step. In the 1900s, the age of the specialist, a person's success often hinged on their depth of experience. In fact, specialists were revered; the greater your degree of specialty, the higher your status. We had moved away from an appreciation of the broadly educated individual. Being a specialist carried a great deal more cache. Because the world was compartmentalized, it made sense that people who had in-depth knowledge and experience in each compartment were needed and had an important role to play. There is plenty of evidence that this was not, even then, the best way of working. Specializing can limit thinking and creativity, not to mention our ability to understand another's perspective, to join forces and to build on one another's ideas.

In spite of this, because our world was hierarchical and compartmentalized and did not experience our present degree of high-paced change, we got by effectively enough working as a collection of specialists, each having our own area of expertise. It worked because specialization was aligned with the "way" of the world at that time. But an interconnected world requires something entirely different. Although having depth of knowledge in one particular area is still important, it is no longer enough. We must also be widely knowledgeable. A wide and current knowledge base is essential to being in step in a fast-changing world. To develop partnerships, work in cross-functional teams, find jobs, be an interesting person others want to connect with—you can't get by without diverse knowledge.

When we work with companies to help them develop strategic plans, we often lead the planning group through an environmental scanning process in which they examine the components of the world around them. They identify significant changes or happenings in each segment, and then look for emerging trends that could either directly or indirectly influence their business. The degree of success of the process depends upon how informed the group is. If the group is well informed, it will extract valuable knowledge from the information.

You, too, must be an environmental scanner, and turn the information you gather into knowledge. You may, for example, be well informed about the best-seller list. You may be able to tell your friends on a weekly basis which are the top five Google trends in people's buying habits, which may be interesting information, but how does it become knowledge? If, when you examine the list every week, you begin to see trends that have longevity, you may have developed some useful knowledge that moves from speculation to assumption based on data. What might the trend you identify suggest to you if you are developing a new product, creating a marketing plan or choosing a new career direction? Not every piece of information holds potential knowledge that will be personally useful, but many do.

Most of us must practice to develop this knowledge-gleaning skill. It requires that we don't just ask "What does that report, article or piece of information say?", but rather "What does it *mean*?" "Have I noticed other pieces of information that say something similar?" "Am I identifying a trend, and, if so, what might that mean to whatever I am doing now, or plan to do next?"

It is important also to be able to separate fads from trends. Fads are short-lived and won't be around long enough to be useful in the long term. Trends, on the other hand, are long term—at least five to ten years in duration. The popularity of styles of music and fashion fall under the heading of fads. In contrast, the shift in traditional gender roles in our society, the move to alternative medicine and healthier eating, online shopping vs bricks and mortar, e-books vs hard copies, 24/7 access to news, the significant rise of social media, the evolution of the sharing economy, and the search for spirituality and higher values are just a handful of examples of trends significantly affecting the way we live and work.

Once you are in tune with the world around you and are able to identify patterns and their forward movement, you can better make decisions for today. Once you have projected a trend into the future and played it out in your mind, you can grasp opportunities before others are even aware of their presence and make decisions for the future. Every enterprise you undertake will be more effective.

Take the evolution of the sharing economy, for example. Peer-to-peer markets have emerged as alternative suppliers of goods and services that are giving traditional businesses and well-established industries are run for their money. You have likely used some of these massive brands like Ebay, TaskRabbit and Uber.

Joe Gebbia and Brian Cheskey are New Renaissance people who capitalized on the sharing economy to the tune of $25 billion US. In 2007, Gebbia and Cheskey were struggling to pay their rent when they had the idea to offer sleeping accommodation on three airbed mattresses in their living room in San Francisco when there were no hotel vacancies due to a popular design conference that week. The next day the two created their website airbedandbreakfast.com, and six days later they had three guests sleeping on their living room floor. Not only did Gebbia and Cheskey make enough money to pay their rent that month, they made lifelong friends and quickly realized the potential of their idea to help people around the world to connect, "share housing, save money, and meet cool people" by offering a creative and affordable alternative to hotels. Gebbia and Cheskey weren't fueled by simply creating a service, they were fueled by the desire to create meaningful experiences and a sense of community by connecting people around the world through their service, now known as Airbnb.

"We were at a point professionally where we were very ready to pursue our own idea. We were anxious though, like waiting in line for a roller coaster. We didn't know exactly what was ahead, but we knew we were in for a ride."[2]

Gebbia and Chesky quickly began seeking out the perfect opportunity to launch their new idea and found it: the 2008 Democratic National Convention in Denver Colorado where hotel accommodation was sure to be sold out. They launched their new site two weeks prior to the convention, and within a week had 800 listings. Pretty impressive. But they weren't making any money. Enter Obamo O's and Cap'n McCain cereal boxes, Gebbia and Chesky's out of the "cereal box" idea to leverage the "breakfast" in airbedandbreakfast.com while capitalizing on the buzz surrounding the convention. They sold one thousand cereal boxes on their website for $40 each, earning a profit of almost $30,000 which they invested into their business. Powered by the $30,000 and a pile of credit cards, they began seeking investors — who all turned them down. Until 2010, that is, when they secured their first major round of funding and could finally launch a booking fee to monetize the site and begin generating revenue. The rest as they say, is history. Within a few short years, Airbnb grew from a small start up to a global phenomenon where guests can rent almost any type of accommodation anywhere in the world. Whether you want a treehouse in Costa Rica, a cave in Sydney, an entire Fiji island or simply a room in Toronto to attend your second cousin's wedding, you can find it on Airbnb. Since 2008 it has expanded to over 190 countries, with over 60 million

[2] Allentrepreneur (n.d). Retrieved from https://allentrepreneur.wordpress.com/2009/08/26/travel-like-a-human-with-joe-gebbia-co-founder-of-airbnb/

guests using the service, and is now valued at approximately US $31 billion in 2017.

Gebbia and Chesky's success is fueled by their ability to tap into emerging trends and incorporate them into Airbnb. For instance, the need to create a scenario for "everyone to win" is the cornerstone of the sharing economy. At Airbnb, everyone wins, from the guests who get personable hospitality at a more affordable price to hosts who receive extra income from renting out their space, to the communities who attract tourists to traditionally non-touristy areas. And perhaps the trend that has had the greatest impact on Airbnb's success is the growing desire for connection and uniqueness. Gebbia and Chesky tapped into the desire for people to have a personal experience more embedded with the destination of choice's culture and community in a very real and personal way, at an affordable cost.

> *I'd rather fail doing something that I love, than always wonder what could have been.*
>
> Brian Chesky, Founder Airbnb

Marcia Kilgore is also a New Renaissance person.[3] She left her hometown of Outlook, Saskatchewan—and its two thousand residents—for New York when she was 18 years old. There, in one of the most competitive cities in the world, and by the age of 28, she became a successful businesswoman as owner and operator of Bliss, one of New York's most popular spas. She started in business by giving facials in one room in Soho and doing everything else, including dragging towels to the local laundromat at midnight. Within a few years her luxury spa, Bliss occupied two trendy floors was booked

---

[3] *Maloney, N. (2017) "How Marcia Kilgore is Changing the Face of Beauty, One Brand at a Time" Retrieved from* https://www.vanityfair.com/style/2017/12/how-marcia-kilgore-is-changing-the-business-of-beauty-one-brand-at-a-time

months in advance—often by Hollywood actresses such as Demi Moore and Uma Thurman.

Remarkably, just three years later Bliss was sold for US$30 million and Kilgore moved on to found and creatively lead three more successful companies: Soap and Glory, Fitflop and Beauty Pie.

Kilgore is a natural environmental scanner with an ability to tune in to current needs and tastes of consumers.

Gebbia, Chesky, and Kilgore are superb environmental scanners with the ability to tune into the needs and tasks of consumers. They recognized early on the experiential trend that was emerging at the end of 20th century. People did not just want to purchase something, whether a product, lodging, or a treatment, they wanted an experience. Their astounding success is due to the fact that they tuned in, not only to one trend, but to several—and catered to each in just the right proportion.

Timing Is Everything

Every living thing has a life cycle. People are never static; they are in perpetual motion. So are ideas, trends, products, projects. They are either expanding as they move toward a peak—or strongest and fullest moment—or they are contracting as they move with depleted energy toward the end of their cycle. The end of the cycle may not necessarily mean that the behaviors and interest attached to the trend are dead but may have simply become a norm which means that everyone is now on board and opportunities are fewer and competition greater.

A key to success is being able to identify a trend some time before it reaches its peak, but not so early as to be too far ahead of the curve. If no one else can see at least a hint of whatever you envision, it's pretty hard to garner others' interest. So as the old saying goes, "Timing is everything." If you time it well you can enjoy the fruits when the energy is strong—before, during and immediately after the peak.

True trends are sufficiently long term that insightful environment scanners can usually identify or label them. However, another challenge is to catch the ideas and products that emerge from and reflect the trends at the right moment, because their individual life cycles are much shorter. A product, for example may be influenced by several trends, including social and economic ones, as well as by its competition.

Depending on how these variables come together, the life cycle may speed up or slow down. Good timing results from environmental scanning combined with intuition. People who jump into something at an early stage are, for the most part, going on intuition; there is not yet enough evidence to make a decision based on logic. Dyson, Gebbia, Chesky and Kilgore were all fueled by their strong belief that their ideas would come to fruition – against all logic and visible evidence.

As the pace of change accelerates, so does the life cycle of most new ideas. Timing, therefore, must be precise. Great ideas today can be passé tomorrow. We must then be able and willing to change direction, to shape and develop ideas on the go, and to be open to making adjustments until the last possible minute.

There are times when we both likely drive our editors crazy. A book evolves over many months, and sometimes longer. As it does, the world for which it is being created is experiencing both subtle and dramatic changes. It is a challenge to get the book out right when the *need* for the book is entering its pre-peak period. In addition, the packaging, including cover graphics and title, has its own cycle. It is not uncommon for either of us to have a strong feeling that something we agreed upon earlier is not as good an idea as it once seemed. The idea might have been a strong one if we had been putting books on the shelves the day we thought of it, but we caught it too late in its cycle.

One of us may sense, for example, that a title agreed upon two months ago, and that the editor subsequently "sold" internally with enthusiasm, is no longer "right." We often don't have a lot of proof that we're right. We can perhaps mention a trend or two that seem to be emerging (again, not as yet proven). While there is little evidence to support the feeling, there is lots of evidence that titles similar to the one first chosen, sold extremely well, which is what supported the decision to go with the original title in the first place. Did those books perhaps enter the market at the right spot on the curve? Were other variables at work in determining the success of the other books? The editor then has to try to explain to other members of the publishing team that his author "feels" that what appears to be a perfectly good title—one based on solid evidence—will no longer work. He and I both face the possibility of looking like we haven't a clear direction or are downright flaky, or worse, the possibility of being wrong and putting out a book with a title that doesn't appeal to the market.

This is precisely the dilemma confronted by everyone who has a "feeling" about something while it is in the early stages of its cycle. They are using information, but it is often in the form of unarticulated subtle messages that are picked up by intuition not logic. But because there is no proof, there is risk. They may be misreading signals. They may be wrong. They could be missing the mark altogether. We know nothing lasts forever, but where is it at this moment in its life cycle?

That's the challenge, and for many the excitement, of today's world. Risk-taking, always part and parcel of success, is elevated today, whether you are making a decision about a job (What's the life cycle of the industry, the company, your particular skill or function?), investing in a product, purchasing a product or starting a business.

But we can reduce the risk. With practice, we can more astutely read the environment—and develop our intuition, as we will discuss later.

Some read the environment instinctively. Most of us have to practice. It can be fun to scan information regularly, look for patterns and identify possible trends. You may immediately be able to apply the knowledge you gain. At the very least, you will impress those around you with your insight—and that alone can have huge paybacks. There is no doubt that at some point your knowledge will allow you to recognize opportunities and act on them with greater success.

WORKOUTS FOR EMBRACING THE NEW RENAISSANCE

See Appendix A: for more information on How to Approach the Workouts.

1: Broaden Your Knowledge Base

1. List the programs you watch and the radio or podcasts you listen to regularly that provide information or knowledge.
2. For each program you have listed, find the knowledge category below that best fits, and put a checkmark beside it.

_____ News and current events	_____ Sports
_____ Science	_____ Health and well-being
_____ General interest	_____ Economics
_____ Business and finance	_____ Technology
_____ Arts and literature	_____ Politics
	_______Entertainment

3. Repeat the above considering your reading material both off and on-line.

_____ News and current events	_____ Sports
_____ Science	_____ Health and well-being
_____ General interest	_____ Economics
_____ Business and finance	_____ Technology
_____ Arts and literature	_____ Politics
	_____ Entertainment

4. Examine your results. Do you access a broad range of information or knowledge? Where are the knowledge gaps?
5. List additional sources you can access to broaden and better balance your knowledge base.
6. Keep your eyes open for new sources of knowledge.

2: Avoid Tunnel Vision

We are naturally attracted to information about our own areas of expertise or personal interest. Our knowledge grows almost organically in these areas. But unless we have broad interests, the results can be in-depth knowledge of limited subjects.

Importantly we often ignore opportunities to learn from information that doesn't match that which we have already decided is "right." This is strongly at play when it comes to elections and referendums, but applies to any area in which we have strong feelings and have firmly made up our minds. We look for information that confirms what we already believe and look for ways to discredit what doesn't fit our view of things.

1. Challenge yourself for at least one week to learn about topics that you have no interest in whatsoever.
2. Watch an informational program or read an article that you would normally click past.
3. Read an article that disagrees with your point of view and look for at least one point that perhaps makes you reflect at least a little on your own position.
4. Make the above practices a regular habit.

3: Become a Learning Organization of One

Successful organizations embrace the concept of the "learning organization." They know that learning must be constant if they are to respond effectively to change.

Successful individuals never miss an opportunity to learn. They question others; they read widely; they access all sources of information; they assess their own performance.

Consider what *you* learned today.

1. Jot down a list of what you have learned within the last 24 hours.
2. Check whether you missed anything by considering what you could have learned from each of the following:
   - Others
   - Media

- You successes and failures
- Formal education and training

3. Are you intellectually richer than you were 24 hours ago? If you see room for improvement, identify learning opportunities that you can better tap and make a commitment to doing so.

4: Know Thyself

Knowledge is power. Knowledge about ourselves is the most powerful of all — if we choose to use it.

1. List personal traits that you know at times hinder you. If you are having difficulty coming up with them, think about comments on performance reviews that you dismissed as biased or unfair, or ask people who know you well and will be honest.
2. Work on one trait at a time. Commit to being on the watch for it presenting itself. Assess yourself at the end of the day. Did the trait slip out? If so, replay the incident in your mind. Replace your unfavourable behaviour with a more positive and effective one. Be aware of the feeling when you replace the less productive trait with a more positive behaviour. How does it feel to behave differently?

If you have some stubborn trait that you wish to correct use this exercise regularly. Spending ten minutes a day focusing on improved behaviours can make a tremendous difference to your relationships, your stress level and how you see yourself.

Law #2

WALK FAST ON THIN ICE

"When walking on thin ice, you have to walk fast." This is an old Russian proverb that holds an important message for our time. Thin ice has become a permanent condition. It behooves each of us to learn how to cross it.

We know the pace of change that we are experiencing today will not decelerate. The future of companies can change overnight; our economy's increased sensitivity to a sneeze anywhere in the world will continue. The significance for each of us is that we will never feel secure in our jobs.

If you are a risk-taker by nature, you have an advantage. You are at home on thin ice. But simply being comfortable working in an environment in which nothing is sure does not guarantee success. Walking fast on thin ice requires skill and, more importantly, balance.

Travel Lightly

Every day we must respond sensitively and speedily in an unpredictable environment. Those who travel lightly can respond most quickly. But people insist on carrying old baggage that weighs them down and severely limits their ability to respond. That baggage contains the memories and emotions of experience that in some way hurt us. The emotions can suddenly be triggered by new events—even though the baggage is weeks, and even years, old.

A Sufi story tells of two monks who were walking along a river bank. A tiny woman approached them and asked if one of them would carry her across the river. "Oh, no, we can't do that!" exclaimed one. "It wouldn't be proper."

The second monk looked down at the woman, who was desperate to cross the river but risked being swept away if she attempted it on her own. "I'll carry you across," he said.

"But you can't do that," protested the first monk. "It isn't right."

All three crossed the river, the second monk carrying the woman. They left her on the other side of the river and continued their journey. Repeatedly the concerned monk muttered, "You shouldn't have done that. It was wrong to carry the woman."

Finally, after some time, his companion said, "I set that woman down a long time ago. Why are you still carrying her?"

Most of us are still carrying around distressful experiences that everyone else involved has forgotten about and that now have no significance. But we just can't let go. And that weight, in a small or large way, limits our capabilities.

John, for example, was once cheated by a partner, someone he liked and trusted. He had thought they were friends. Every time he remembers what happened, he feels not only emotional pain, but real physical pain in his stomach. He now has difficulty trusting anyone. Often his hesitancy to develop partnerships means opportunities lost. When he is in a situation in which he is working with others, he looks over their shoulder, both slowing down the project and preventing trust from developing. This fear of trusting has frequently handicapped him.

> *To be wronged is nothing unless you continue to remember it.*
>
> Confucius

Kathryn once made a fool of herself, she believes, in a presentation she gave several years ago. The heat of embarrassment washes over her every time she thinks of it. Now she refuses to make presentations. While she possesses the skills, others assume she lacks the ability and confidence, and she is missing opportunities to raise her profile in the company. She imagines that everyone remembers her botched presentation and that it colors their view of her. If she asked anyone about that presentation, undoubtedly they would respond, "What presentation are you talking about?"

Some people are conscious of the weight they carry. They live over and over again the embarrassment of an experience, and feel over and over again the negative emotions attached to it. With each replay they deride themselves a little more, and renew their determination that "it will never happen again, no matter what the cost."

Others are not as conscious of the event, but the conditioning remains. "Never let anyone make a fool of you." "Don't do anything unless you can do it perfectly." The burden still weighs us down.

Consider the experiences you carry with you. What have people said or done to you in the past that has hurt and angered you? What have people said or done for you in the past that made you feel good? Which list is longer and was easier to recall? If it was the former, consider how to lighten your load.

Sometimes burdens, although weighty, have become familiar companions, and we hesitate to release them. Those who have learned to walk fast on thin ice identify their burdens, and then get rid of them. They make sure they are traveling lightly.

Winner's Tip: Getting rid of old negative memories makes room for new positive ones.

Get Out of Your Way

You can't walk fast on thin ice if you are always tripping yourself up. And you will certainly trip yourself up more often than not if you don't have the right attitude. The dictionary defines attitude as "a way of looking at life; a way of thinking, feeling or behaving." Attitude is made up of thoughts, feelings and behaviors, and each of these three things has a direct impact on the results we create in our life and work. The good news is, is that every individual has the power to choose their thoughts and behavior. Winners are experts at practicing the art of mindfulness; they are aware of their thinking patterns and how the thoughts they have impact how they feel and how they behave, they know without a doubt that their thoughts have a direct impact on the results they create. Winners know that it is not what happens to them in life that creates their experience but how they *respond* to what happens, and therefore they can create whatever experience they want by choosing the most productive thoughts and behaviors.

When we ask people what is preventing them from being as successful as they would like to be, the answers we most frequently hear are the following:

- the economy
- competition
- my boss
- lack of experience
- lack of a particular skill or knowledge base

Seldom do we hear "me" or "my behavior."

But when we ask managers what, in their experience, is preventing people from getting ahead, the most common responses relate to attitude or behavior. The barriers to our success or our *greater* success are most often ourselves. We need to get out of our own way—and let ourselves succeed.

A significant step to getting out of your own way is being conscious of how your thoughts directly impact your behavior and your outcomes. The average person has about fifty thousand thoughts per day[4], and what is even more amazing is that 98% of them are exactly the same as we had the day before. Exactly the same as the day before! And, what is still even more astonishing is that, close to 80%[5] of our thoughts *are negative*. Almost 80% of the time *we are thinking negatively about ourselves*, about another person, or about a situation, or worrying about the future or dwelling on the past. So if we have negative thoughts 80% of the time, how are we feeling 80% of the time?

---

[4] Reference. (n.d). Retrieved from https://www.reference.com/world-view/many-thoughts-per-minute-cb7fcf22ebbf8466#

[5] Psychology Today. (n.d.) Retrieved from: https://www.psychologytoday.com/blog/wired-success/201305/do-self-affirmations-work-revisit

NEGATIVE, of course. We also know from research that these thoughts have a powerful effect on us. They affect our attitude, our physiology, and our motivation to act. Our negative thoughts actually control our behavior. Take polygraph tests for example, your body reacts to your thoughts, changing your temperature, heart rate, blood pressure, breathing rate, muscle tension. When you are hooked up to a lie detector and are asked a question such as "Did you take the money?", your hands will get colder, your heart will beat faster, your blood pressure will go up, your breathing will get faster, your muscles will get tighter, and your hands will sweat if you did take the money and you lie about it. These kinds of physiological changes not only occur when you're lying, but also in reaction to every thought you think. Every cell in your body is affected by every thought you have. Negative thoughts affect your body negatively – weakening you, making you sweat and making you uptight. Positive thoughts affect your body in a positive way – making you more relaxed, centered and alert.

This brings to mind the quote from Aristotle, "We are what we repeatedly do. Excellence then, is not an act, but a habit." If thoughts are habitual (98% of them are the same as the day before), and thoughts drive behaviors, you had better make sure that you are thinking the right thoughts to create habits that lead to excellence in your life and work. If you are not achieving what you want in life, it is more likely than not the result of falling into a negative thinking pattern. Winners are aware of the thoughts they have and consciously choose to actively create thoughts that will lead to feelings, behaviors and habits that are most important to achieving the outcomes they want.

Most of the thoughts and behaviors that trip us up are familiar companions. We are well aware of them, but have chosen not to change them or didn't realize that we had the power to do it: thoughts that promote self-doubt and fear, holding on to the past, a quick temper, a too-direct style that offends others, a penchant for detail that others see as nit-picking, a tendency to keep information to ourselves. It's important to acknowledge these self-defeating behaviors, but that is only half the battle.

When business leaders are asked to identify what they see as the key success factors today, a common response is one very much like that of Steven Quesnelle, Partner at Sacred Cow Company: "Self awareness. Putting yourself under a microscope, so that you understand yourself and understand people around you, is essential."

In an interconnected world that depends on teams and partnerships, behaviors that trip you up also directly affect others' performance. Teammates and partners are much quicker to insist on behavioral changes than were managers in the past.

Apply the Learning Internally

Some of the most important learning we must undertake, and often the most difficult to grasp and use, is self-knowledge. What are our own strengths and weaknesses? What changes do we personally have to make, within ourselves and perhaps in our environment, if we are to be able to use our winner instinct?

> *When the rate of change outside exceeds the rate of change inside, the end is in sight.*
>
> Jack Welch, former Chairman and CEO, General Electric

Welch was referring to organizations but applies powerfully to the individual. Each of us has had so much change imposed on us that the reflex response to "Are you changing?" is "Of course!" Further discussion, however, often reveals that we are not doing things any differently. Consider your own situation. If you are in the workforce, you are probably using more technology, attending more meetings, updating more skills and taking on new and additional responsibilities. But how are you approaching these changes? You may attend more meetings but respond in those meetings as you always have. You may use new technology but not apply new thinking to its use.

Anyone who is managing to get by today is coping with change in one way or another. Many are using the run faster-and-keep-smiling technique. We can, however, only cope for so long and with so much, no matter how hard we work or how positive our attitude. As we know, accelerated change is here to stay. Those who will be winners are able not just to cope, but to make appropriate *adjustments.* Adjusting means changing the *way* we do things; it means changing ourselves.

Susan was a data manager. She was bright and forward looking, and she could see that the near future would mean fewer jobs and less opportunity for advancement in her organization. She took the initiative to take courses that put her ahead technologically, as well as courses that ensured she was on top of the latest ideas and systems in her field. She invested time and money into hiring a specialist to help her create a resume that drew a clear picture of an experienced, capable, skilled, knowledgeable and proactive individual. She applied for new positions that were being created as her company reorganized and even tried to create a job for herself when she spotted a need. She prepared carefully for each interview. Each time, she was complimented on what she had to offer as well as her impressive resume but she never got the job.

In a painful examination of what went wrong, she recognized that although she had proactively done much of what is required for success today, she hadn't done anything about the most important component of what she had to offer: herself as a co-worker and team member. She was doing many *different things,* but she wasn't truly doing *things differently.* She hadn't changed in a personal way.

She realized that she had ignored the input she had received time and again in performance review sessions. "Susan," various managers had told her, "many of the staff find it difficult to work with you. You are seen to be very controlling, insisting that things be done as you see fit and within your own time frame." Susan had felt that a few jealous people were complaining about her, but on some level she knew that she did communicate her need to control and that that created conflict. It was even evident in her home life, but her husband loved her enough to accept her style and let her be the driver. Fellow employees did not have the same tolerance.

Changing her long-term controlling behavior was difficult for Susan. She felt stress when she relinquished control. With much effort and coaching to support her, she made inroads, but it was difficult for her to change others' negative perception of her—one built up over several years. Susan had to begin looking for opportunities elsewhere, hoping her reputation wouldn't precede her.

Most of us are aware of the personal habits or traits that limit us. We may recognize them ourselves, or have been lucky enough to have a manager or colleague who cared enough to undertake the usually difficult task of giving us feedback. Too seldom do we act on such valuable information.

Others find it hard to let go of the "old" way of doing things. Intellectually, they may be saying yes to the change, but behaviorally, they don't make the effort. In many organizations, I see that the entire game has been changed. It's as though the participants once played hockey, but are now playing football. Intellectually, employees recognize that this is a new game and have even been trained in how to play it. But inevitably some people don't score as often or easily as they once ; when things don't work as well as they used to, they blame the new game. They grumble that the turf doesn't work as well as the ice did, and that you could move faster on skates.

They don't recognize that the problem is their firm grip on "the old."

> *Every exit is an entry somewhere else.*
>
> Tom Stoppard

Others attempt to take on the new, but hold on to the past as well. Leslie remembers an opportunity she once had to attend a Shango ceremony on the island of Grenada that exemplifies this. Shango is an African based religion practiced in some parts of the Caribbean. "It was a dramatic experience for the uninitiated: driving through a pitch-black night up narrow, winding mountain roads, and then walking along paths through jungle-like growth, following the sound of the drums until we came to a clearing lit by a fire. Dancers and their shadows filled the space in front of a small wooden house perched on stilts.

The Shango priest and many followers were gathered for several nights of drum music, dancing and rituals. This ceremony had a particular purpose. The house was believed to be possessed by a spirit which had brought the woman who lived there much bad luck. The ceremony was meant to entice the spirit from the house.

The owner, with typical Grenadian hospitality, invited us into the tiny one-room house, dimly—and to us, eerily—lit by a kerosene lamp. On a table were offerings to the troublesome spirit, including different foods, particularly sweet cakes that were purported to be the god Shango's favorite (and also happened to be mine). But something else in the room caught my attention. In one corner, obviously a centerpiece, was an altar to the Virgin Mary, around which were arranged candles and incense. This woman, like many who practice Shango and similar religions, was hanging on to both the belief and practices of her roots and those of Christianity that had been introduced long ago. Her belief in Shango was deep, but on the other hand, what if Christianity held the truth? We often see much the same behavior in people trying to succeed in the corporate world. They go through the motions required of the new but deep down, part of them still believes in the old which often hinders their ability to fully embrace the change that is being introduced.

"Old," however, is not always bad. The New Renaissance person is a discerning *change agent.* They do not throw out everything that is not perceived to be the latest concept or technique, but recognize classics that will always be relevant and mix them comfortably with new practices.

Walking on thin ice, and making progress without falling through, requires not only speed but carefully placed steps. This is not a time to be setting ourselves on autopilot, and yet that is just what most people do. We bolt out of bed in the morning and hurl ourselves into the challenges of the day, behaving exactly as we did yesterday and the day before that and the day before that. Autopilot served us well enough in an age when conditions seldom changed, providing our behaviors were appropriate. But today, ice conditions, direction and strength of wind, temperature and so on are constant variables. We must select our responses much more consciously.

Getting to the Heart of the Matter

Did you know that people with average IQs outperform those with the highest IQs 70% of the time? This statistic has thrown a wrench into the belief that IQ and book smarts are the primary drivers of success. Winners however, don't need decades of research to intuitively know that IQ has little to do with success. This brings us to an essential element in thriving in a volatile environment — the heart of winner instinct. The ease with which you work in concert with the 6 New Laws of Success depends greatly on your personal mix of behaviors and actions. And the right mix at the right time results in the balance you require to effectively respond to the world around you. In other words, it determines your success.

Our behavioral choices fall essentially into two categories: vertical or task-oriented preferences, and horizontal or process-oriented preferences. In the old world, you could go to work and, to a great extent, do the following:

- live in your own cubicle
- focus on your own job
- make purely logical decisions based on your own experience or your own research
- hoard information if you chose to, and not bother to share it
- assume that the education and training you brought to the job would last a lifetime
- let other people fend for themselves
- participate in meetings if you felt like it
- assume that the success of the team you were part of was someone else's problem, as long as you did your part well
- firmly hold on to your own paradigms of what works and what doesn't
- focus on the job, and not worry too much about the people
- be more concerned about getting the job done than *how* it was done
- be narrowly informed or even uninformed, and still succeed

Task Preferences (Vertical)		Process Preferences (Horizontal)
Independent Works best independently	•------------------•	**Interactive** Works best with others
Detached Focuses on data	•------------------•	**Attached** Focuses on people/ feelings/beliefs
Inward-Looking Focuses on detail and the concrete	•------------------•	**Outward-Looking** Focuses on the big picture and the theoretical
Logical Is driven by reason	•------------------•	**Intuitive** Is driven by an inner sense and creativity
Convergent Has the "answer" Brings things to closure	•------------------•	**Divergent** Searches for the "answer" Opens things up

For more detail see Appendix C.

These vertical or task-oriented behaviors, compatible with a vertical society and workplace, worked well enough at one time.

Our precarious, changeable, knowledge-based world, however, functions very differently from the old one. It works horizontally rather than vertically. It is interconnected, flat and fluid. In order to be in concert with our world today, you must be able to demonstrate not only task-oriented behaviors but their opposites as well. Success requires spending a great deal of time and effort connecting with others effectively; being creative, responsive, outward-looking, highly informed, and flexible. At the same time, we need to be able to move to a task-oriented mode when needed: use logic, pay attention to detail, close down discussion, and bring decision-making processes to closure.

The knowledge-based society is an age of paradox, combining task orientation (focusing on getting across the ice) with the new-world process orientation (focusing on how you make the crossing). It is a constant dance: one step toward process, and one step back to toward task. To be in step at any particular moment, you must be conscious of whether your movements are in sync with the constantly changing world.

> *To lead in times of change means to focus as much on the process as on the final product and to profit from the adventure of being en route and living in between.*[6]
>
> Barbara Forisha-Kovac

If on our trek across the ice we hit a spot that is thinner, or the wind picks up, we need to respond differently in order to stay on our feet and move forward with the care that is required.

Winner's Tip: We seldom just **maintain** balance, but constantly make adjustments in an attempt to **achieve** balance.

Some people by nature are more task-oriented, others are more process-oriented, and a smaller percentage are equally comfortable in either mode. Those individuals who are task-oriented have a great deal to contribute to the knowledge-based society, but have a difficult time *making* their contribution because they are often out of step. They may be busy telling others, who expect to be

[6] Barbara Forisha-Kovach. *The Flexible Organization.* Edgewood Cliffs, NJ: Prentice-Hall, 1984.

allowed to make their own decisions, what to do; insisting on "just the facts" in decision-making, when facts alone are inadequate; or focusing on details while the competition is cornering the market by understanding the big picture.

People who are process-oriented are, for the most part, in step with the new requirements, and can give a beautiful performance that appears in sync with the way the world works today. Their success is often thwarted, however, by their inability to pay attention to details, move things along quickly and bring things to closure.

Many people don't respond thoughtfully to the events of the day but react with familiar behaviors and mind-sets. You can usually predict their reaction in various situations. They may be the ones who speak first at a meeting, or play devil's advocate; they may prefer to wait for as much information as possible before making a decision, or want to make gut-level decisions; they may have to be extremely well prepared and dot every *i* and cross every *t,* or they be quite happy winging it. Each of these responses may be appropriate sometimes, but none is always appropriate.

A fortunate few can get away with working on autopilot because they are synthesizers—people who are as comfortable in a task mode as in a process mode—who move comfortably and intuitively back and forth, as needed, between the two sets of behaviors. But most of us are *not* synthesizers and have potential handicaps as a result.

Find Balance through Growth – Leslie's Experience

I was married, had two children, and had had several careers before I faced my biggest personal handicap. It took some time before I began to effectively overcome it. In fact, I am still working on it.

Most Achilles' heels require lifetime management, although the vigilance required greatly lessens as time goes on.

When it came to my Achilles' heel, I was a slow learner because, like most people, I was much more comfortable working the way I had always done; I had always "gotten by" working that way. Most importantly, I hadn't made a specific commitment to deal with my Achilles' heel and so hadn't put in place a plan to make the required changes happen. As a result, it took me two years to make the progress that I could have made in two months.

If there is such a thing as an unforgivable sin, I'm convinced it's not applying the knowledge we gained. Long before I developed the Task Process model I recognized that, by nature, I had a strong preference for the Independent mode. Almost all of the Independent descriptors reflected the behaviors and preferences that came most naturally to me:

- I preferred to work independently
- I worked well on my own
- I tended to solve problems in isolation
- I didn't like talking about myself

Now, these natural tendencies are not the most useful for someone trying to build a business as a consultant to leaders and teams! A basic success requirement was for me to be able to sell myself. Independent consultants are both the salesperson and the product being sold, in that what they are selling is their own knowledge and skills. This is not an easy task for individuals who do not like talking about themselves.

This particular aspect of my Independent trait limited me in a variety of other ways, although at first I didn't recognize the culprit. For my very first television appearance, I was asked to do a call-in- style talk show on how to be successful in the workplace. The host, known for his aggressive manner, actually attempted to put me at ease with a casual opening question. "Bendaly," he said. "That's an interesting name. Where does it come from?" I froze. "He's asking about *me*!" I had been expecting impersonal questions about what *others* could do to be successful at work. I became flustered and mumbled, "Well, it's a long story," and he wisely moved on.

But my confidence was shot in the first few seconds of a half-hour show. I somehow struggled through, but I remember driving away from the station chastising myself: "Well, Leslie, if you are going to blow it, why not blow it in front of thousands of people?"

It was a long time, however, before I benefited from that experience. All I recognized was "I blew it!" I hadn't yet identified my Achilles' heel enough to recognize the role that it had played in what my mind came to call That Show. Gradually, I came to recognize how my Independent nature could undermine my success, how much harder I had to work because of it, and what I could do to manage it and thereby achieve in spite of it.

Remember, however, that every strong preference also has its advantages. In my case, for example, an Independent nature allowed me to leave the corporate environment and strike out on my own.

Personal growth tends to be something to which everyone responds, "Yes, of course, that's obvious, everyone has to do that." And then they move on to something else. It always seems easier and more comfortable to change something or someone *else.*

WORKOUTS FOR WALKING FAST ON THIN ICE

See Appendix A: How to Approach the Workouts.

1: Check Your Baggage

Try to identify the old baggage that is inhibiting your progress.

1. List old resentments that still linger in the back (or the forefront) of your mind. Also, assign yourself the task of watching for old baggage over the next week. Often if you overreact to a situation, your reaction has been triggered by past experiences that you have not resolved.
2. Once you have collected your baggage, try this technique that works for many people. Write each resentment on a separate piece of paper (8 1/2-by-11 inch). Crumple each sheet into a ball, one by one, and toss each dramatically (with emotion!) into the garbage. If any are particularly heavy burdens, you may wish to create an even more symbolic gesture: burn them.

As you get rid of each piece, tell yourself that you won't allow it to burden you again.

3. Be vigilant. Every time a piece of old baggage reappears, quickly and firmly wipe it from your mind.

2: Keep Moving

Standing still on thin ice is fatal. You must keep forging ahead. Are you moving ahead? Are you moving fast enough?

1. Think about the past week:
   - Did you say or think "That won't work" and dismiss an idea without thoroughly exploring it? (Remember, the greater our expertise in an area, the more difficult it can be for us to recognize new and better ways.)

- Did you make a contact with someone who is forward thinking?
- Did you stop to assess your effectiveness, and then try to find better ways of doing things?
- Did you access any sources to update yourself professionally?
- Did you learn from problems?
- Did you broaden your general knowledge?
- Did you do some homework on your competitors?

2. List anything else you did to keep moving ahead.

Some successful people automatically work these activities into their daily routine. If you don't, schedule a few minutes, several times a week, to do the things you see as most important to ensure that you are not standing still.

3. The Art of Mindfulness – managing your inner dialogue
   Use these tips to become aware of your inner dialogue and to practice replacing negative and unproductive dialogue with more productive thoughts that will contribute directly to more positive feelings, beliefs and direct action towards your goals.
   - Find time throughout your day to direct your attention to your inner dialogue. Observe your thoughts objectively as though you are a third party bystander. How are your thoughts making you feel? Do you notice any patterns about yourself and your inner dialogue?
   - Notice how your thoughts are affecting your mood and behavior in the moment. For example, instead of getting sucked into a spiral of negative energy and emotion, instead simply notice what you are telling yourself and thinking about in the moment and how those thoughts are directly impacting how you

feel and behave. Choose to stop the inner dialogue in that moment and pivot to more productive thoughts. Simply choose to instead focus on all that you are grateful for and identify one thing you can do to get yourself into a more positive frame of mind.

- Practice challenging your thoughts by replacing negative ones with more productive ones. This can be accomplished simply by challenging assumptions with questions like, "How do I know this is true?" ; "What's the worst that can happen?" ; "What am I grateful for in this moment?" ; "What can I focus on that is positive and will help me to move forward?"

4. Strengthen your self-image

"Float like a butterfly, sting like a bee. Nobody can beat me, Mohammad Ali."

Muhammad Ali was, and will always be remembered, one of the greatest heavyweight championship boxers of all time, and as one of the most beloved figures of all time.

Ali once said, "It's the repetition of affirmations that leads to belief. And once that belief becomes a deep conviction, things begin to happen." Ali knew, like all winners, that nothing is more important than how you think and feel about yourself.

Self-affirmations were first popularized by French psychologist Emile Coué back in the 1920s and recent studies have shown that self-affirmation has a direct impact on performance, problem solving and stress reduction[39]. Research shows that pausing regularly to think about something that is important to you, that you are grateful for, or that you appreciate, will have a direct impact on your self-esteem, performance and stress.

Use this quick exercise every day to help boost your self-esteem and performance.

Take two minutes at the beginning of every day and:

- Disconnect from technology, take a deep break, and quiet your mind.
- Ask yourself: "What are three things I can appreciate about myself today?"

With this exercise, you will begin to shift your mind's autopilot from dishing out negative self-talk to dishing out positive and productive self-talk.

3: Balancing Your Personal Task/Process Style

1. Complete the Personal Task/Process Style Indicator (*Appendix C)*
2. Consider any dimensions that indicate a strong preference (scores of 17 or more for one dimension of the pair, and 13 or less for the other). Do you already manage these behaviors—that is, do you recognize when to rein in your natural tendencies and respond to a situation as required?
3. When you are under pressure, you are most likely to slip into behaviors that come naturally to you even though they may not be appropriate. If, after reflection, you decide that you do not always manage these behaviors well, develop strategies for doing so. You might try the following:

- Identify the types of situations in which you are most likely to demonstrate these potentially detrimental behaviors. Commit to being vigilant in these situations, and be conscious of how you are responding.

- At the end of each day, do a quick review. Picture what you did and said, and how people reacted to you (or, if this was not evident, how they were probably responding to you). What would you do differently next time?
- Ask a trusted colleague if she sees evidence of your personal preferences, and if your behaviors are ever detrimental to others, to outcomes or to yourself. For example, if you have a high Inward-Looking score, you might acknowledge, "I know I tend to focus on details and may at times overlook the big picture." Then ask questions such as the following: Is this evident to others? What effect does my focus on details have on others or on the outcome? Does it affect how people see me? How? Consider their responses and commit to changing your behavior accordingly.

4: How Your Profile Affects Your Credibility

The following three case studies are included to give you a sense of how our Personal Task/Process Style Profile can affect others' impressions of us, and ultimately our success. Read the cases, then revisit your own profile by considering the questions that follows.

CASE STUDY 1: Marsha Robinson

Personal Task/Process Style Profile

Task-Focused		**Process-Focused**	
Independent	22	Interactive	8
Detached	20	Attached	10
Inward-Looking	19	Outward-Looking	11
Logical	20	Intuitive	10

Convergent	23	Divergent	7

Marsha Robinson is a member of a management team. As her organization has experienced upheaval and change, there has been an increased need for her and her colleagues to work as a team. As the team load has increased, so has the individual load, and managers have been struggling to meet their own personal performance requirements. While the meetings and increased "teamness" were seen as beneficial to the other team members, all of whom had an Interactive preference, Robinson saw these activities as a necessary evil that were eating into her time and were therefore limiting her ability to handle her individual responsibilities effectively. There were always, she felt, more productive ways to use her time.

Robinson was astute enough to recognize that teams were endorsed by senior management and were a fact of life. Therefore, she did not directly resist the team concept and the meetings that went with it, and may not even have been aware that she was quietly—but to her team members, obviously—resisting the new way of doing things. She was the member who always made scheduling meetings difficult. She would always have reasons why she couldn't meet, or ask that a meeting be rescheduled or canceled at the last minute.

Her independent thinking style led to other difficulties. It did not occur to her to bounce ideas off others or to informally share her thinking with people. It did not occur to her to let other team members know that she had been chatting with someone at head office, and to share with others the information she had gained. Robinson communicated only when something was a *fait accompli*. She would frequently not include certain individuals in decision-making processes, even though they had an indirect, and sometimes even direct, stake in the outcome. When decisions had been made in meetings, it was not uncommon for Robinson to mull the decision over afterwards and recognize that something important had been overlooked. Rather than popping in to her colleagues' offices to chat about her ideas, she would send an e-mail to them and to their boss, reworking the decision.

Soon Robinson came to be seen as secretive. It was a common belief that she was planning a power grab in the upcoming restructuring. She was ambitious, but so were most of her teammates. Their ambition was seen as healthy, hers as underhanded.

Robinson's Detached preference caused her to miss the warning signs. Her low Attached score did not mean that she was indifferent to people's feelings; she simply wasn't aware of them. She didn't recognize body language or other verbal and tone-of-voice signs that would have signaled to individuals with higher Attached scores that what they were doing wasn't working. On a few occasions when a team member was sufficiently frustrated to raise concerns about the lack of communication in a meeting, he had usually waited until the issue had become hot. To the highly Detached Robinson, these team members were being overly emotional and needed too much hand-holding. Her high degree of objectivity blocked her from receiving important messages.

Soon Robinson became disempowered as teammates deliberately withheld information from her, challenged her ideas, refused to support her decisions and generally put roadblocks in her way. Robinson was genuinely hurt by what she saw as personal attacks, and bewildered by what was happening.

CASE STUDY 2: Ken Martin

Personal Task/Process Style Profile

Task-Focused		Process-Focused	
Independent	10	Interactive	20
Detached	22	Attached	8
Inward-Looking	9	Outward-Looking	21
Logical	19	Intuitive	11
Convergent	24	Divergent	6

Ken Martin was a member of a sales team. He readily shared his ideas and opinions with others. This might have been an advantage in terms of being interconnected, but his strong scores in two other dimensions—Detached and Convergent—turned a potential asset into a liability.

Martin was a quick thinker, had several years' experience with this company, and had many contacts throughout the industry. The personal experience and knowledge he had gathered along the way, combined with the current intelligence he regularly soaked up meant he had important insights to contribute to his team.

When attending team decision-making meetings, however, Martin's high Convergent preference was strongly in play. He arrived with the best decision—and, as far as he was concerned, the *only* decision—already formulated. He was the first to speak quickly, presenting his "obvious" solution, and expressing impatience when others wanted to take time to explore options. "Why should we go around the bush when the solution is clear?" he would ask in frustration. Others, who were only beginning to grasp the issue and needed more discussion time and would not feel satisfied if they hadn't explored alternatives (those with Attached and Divergent preferences), were equally frustrated with Martin's behavior.

When people issues were raised, for example, some colleagues might not feel comfortable or buy in to a decision. That's when Martin's Detached preference moved into action. "Everyone won't be happy. That's life. We don't have time to hold everyone's hand." And his Convergent nature would add, "Let's just get on with it."

As with Martha Robinson, it wasn't that Martin didn't care about people. It was just that people issues were not the most important factor in his decision-making process—the facts and the task at hand were. His high degree of objectivity meant that he, too, missed the "soft" information that people were sending him about his style. He was oblivious to the fact that his style was turning people off, and as a result his (often good) ideas did not have the impact they deserved.

Sometimes his good ideas were simply rejected by the group. On other occasions, when the group was too tired to bother resisting or the decision was obviously the best one, his idea was accepted—but the lack of commitment on the part of most team members hampered its implementation; thus, the decision never accomplished what it might have.

Martin was constantly frustrated and disappointed, believing that he must be working with a group of incompetent individuals. He couldn't understand when people with less experience and knowledge than he had were chosen for the most interesting projects, or were offered leadership roles. Martin was in many ways a tragic hero, with all kinds of unrealized potential.

CASE STUDY 3: Peter Phillips

Personal Task/Process Style Profile

Task-Focused		**Process-Focused**	
Independent	10	Interactive	20
Detached	22	Attached	18
Inward-Looking	16	Outward-Looking	14
Logical	14	Intuitive	16
Convergent	13	Divergent	17

Peter Phillips was a human resource specialist on a team of highly independent and task-oriented managers. His personal profile matched his job requirements well. He valued people, enjoyed interacting with them, and was sensitive to their needs. His high Interactive and Attached scores meant that he needed interaction himself, and also people to be sensitive to his needs. He looked to his colleagues to fill this need, but as the other members on the management team had Independent and Detached preferences, his needs weren't met.

When meetings weren't called, or issues he felt important weren't dealt with at meetings, his Interactive preference drove him to corner teammates to discussion his concerns about specific issues or the lack of communication in general. Busy colleagues who did not share his need for communication found his visits disruptive. And although Peter did not intend to be negative, the fact that he was constantly raising issues that to others were not important meant that he began to be viewed as negative.

Since he didn't feel he had the information or interaction he needed from his superiors, he also frequented his director's office. The director was another busy individual, whose highest Personal Task/ Process Style Indicator profile scores were also Independent and Detached. He began to see Peter as someone who did his job well but needed too much hand-holding. When a reorganization came along, Peter was sidelined.

The individuals in each of the above case studies had a great deal to offer, but were not able to make an effective contribution because their personal styles were not in balance.

If any of the dimensions of your profile match those of any of the individuals in the case studies, consider whether the difficulties they faced might also apply to you. If so, what changes are required on your part?

Law #3

LIVE WITH PURPOSE AND PASSION

Are you making a life—or just making a living? Winners make a life, and the spin-off benefit is that they also make an excellent living. People who focus too much time and effort on making a living miss much of their life in the process. Does your work bring you fulfillment, or is it time put in, in the hope that the income generated will somehow create the happiness we all pursue?

Or do you have the crazy idea that when you become successful, whatever your definition of success, that you will be happy. The truth is, if you are happy doing whatever you do now, you are more likely to become successful.

One of the most talked-about issues related to personal happiness is balancing personal and work life. We are often approached by people who are exhausted and feel their work life is usurping their personal life. They ask, "I have to work very long hours. I'm often bringing things home, and if on the odd occasion I'm not actually bringing work home, I'm bringing home problems that mentally and emotionally distract me. How can I better separate my home and work life?"

The answer is, they can't. The problem is a real one and there are solutions. But completely separating work and home is not a realistic one.

One of the driving laws of the new world is *interconnectedness.* Compartmentalization does not work in a world in which everything is merging. Trying to build walls is futile. It is fighting against the flow, and only results in greater struggle, which eventually exhausts and defeats you.

The whole idea of separating work and home life is a relatively modern concept that we've come to see as essential to a high-quality life. Our early ancestors did not "go to work" or separate what they did to pay for the essentials from the rest of their lives. Work was part of life. Eventually work became the sacrifice one made in order to earn enough money to live and, for the lucky ones, enough money to play. To work was to toil.

The concept of work as hard and sometimes brutal labor became intensified as the Industrial Revolution pulled people from the farmlands and the cottage industries that could not compete with mass production. They were pushed into the heat, dirt and noise of the joyless factories, or underground into the dark and airless mines that produced the coal that created the steam to drive the monstrous machines. Work and physical labor were synonymous. As white-collar jobs and eventually new technology emerged, the nature of work changed for the most part from a physical activity to an intellectual one. But the predominant mindset held work as drudgery or as something that had to be done for the greatest part of our waking hours in order to, perhaps, experience a little joy in whatever personal time was left. We coped by compartmentalizing our lives, separating work and personal life.

Now our personal and work lives are once again merging. Often they are separated more in our minds than in reality. A growing number of people are telecommuting or have home-based businesses. In these instances, the merging of work, home and personal life is obvious. But even for those in more traditional work modes, it is difficult, if not impossible, to get away from work. Technology ensures our accessibility. The only way many can find time for a vacation is to take work with them; smartphones and iPads are never far from the piña coladas at pool sides and beaches.

The merging of work and personal life is now the norm. Not only is the volume of work flowing over into what we traditionally considered personal space, but the work is, for many, producing increased stress. An unpredictable, hyper-paced world inevitably produces a barrage of stressors over which we have little or no control: the state of the economy, the health of the company for which we work, technological change, competition and often decreased resources. The performance standards are constantly being raised, and competitors, whether external or internal, are on our heels, intent on sprinting into the lead and leaving us in their dust.

The best way to thrive in this environment is *loving* what we do. The good news is that the expectation to work not only for the paycheck, but for the joy in doing the work is becoming more common. Only then can work and personal life merge without our resenting it and subsequently exhausting ourselves. Only then can we be sufficiently strong and resilient to deflect the stressors. Only then can we perform at a level that ensures we will remain relevant in the new world of work and do so with ease not struggle.

"Sure that would be great," you might be thinking. "But I have to earn a living." Know that we are not asking you to ignore reality. If you cannot muster passion for the work you do at the moment start moving forward by applying the other 5 laws and you may be surprised where that takes you.

Be Purposeful

If you are running to get ahead and keep ahead, learn to be purposeful—and soar instead.

Being purposeful means employing our natural gifts and exercising our deep interests. When we are "on purpose," we know that we are doing what we are meant to do.

Dr. Phil Currie, the internationally renowned paleontologist, is likely to be thought of as a lucky guy because he's been successful and has gained recognition doing something he loves.

His passion for dinosaurs and fossils began when he was a child. Through experience and hard work, his passion made him an influential force in his field of vertebrate paleontology. A high point in his career, and one that put him on the cover of *Time,* was his work in confirming, as he says, "not that birds are descended from dinosaurs," but that "birds *are* dinosaurs."[7]

When we once spoke with Currie, he commented that "You've got to be willing to work hard enough to be better than most people." But hard work, he said, isn't enough. "There has to be enthusiasm. If you have enthusiasm—have belief in what you are doing and project it—people will believe you are capable of doing whatever it is you want to do."

His passion and enthusiasm landed him his first job in the field over people who were clearly better qualified. "I went into the interview knowing I had little chance, but at the same time felt that it was meant to be *my* job." His unbridled enthusiasm won the day.

---

[7] *Andrew Purvis. "Call Him Mr. Luck," Time. July 6, 1998.*

If you are good at anything, that is beauty.

Rene Mickenberg, *Taxi Driver Wisdom*

Earning a living by doing what comes naturally ultimately means making a career a vocation. The root of the word vocation is *vocare,* to call. The literal definition of vocation is "calling." It suggests that each of us has a particular talent that we are called upon to use. Vocation suggests purpose in life. Those who take a highly rational approach to life will carefully work to plan, but often that does not result in working to purpose. If we are doing what we have been called to do, it follows that work will be fulfilling and rewarding—personally and financially. Many successful people who have let their hearts lead them to their careers agree. Steven Spielberg has advised people to forget about money, but work hard doing what they love to do. The money, he says, will follow.

Stories abound about people, like Bill Gates, who were driven to success by doing what thrilled them. He once said, "I wrote my first software program when I was thirteen years old . . . and to this day it thrills me to know that if I get a program right, it will always work perfectly, every time, just the way I told it to."[8]

The secret of success is constancy to purpose.

Benjamin Disraeli

Do What Comes Naturally

Those with the greatest passion for their work frequently have known what they were meant to do since they were quite young. In fact, they often were pulled so strongly to their calling that it seemed they

[8] *Bill Gates. The Road Ahead. New York: Penguin, 1995.*

had no choice. In many ways they are the lucky ones; their path has always been obvious to them.

Too often, people spend at least eight hours a day throughout their working lives being something or someone other than themselves. In our workshops, we frequently invite participants to complete an assessment of their personal styles, and often I'm asked, "Should I answer the questions based on who I am at work, or who I am at home?" Day in and day out, people arrive at work but leave their true selves at the door because they don't fit in with the workplace. Little wonder that so many people go home exhausted, or that a large percentage of heart attacks strike on Mondays.

People do not burn out from hard work; they burn out from trying to meet expectations that they were not designed to meet. People who are purposeful are at home at work. They describe a variety of personal experiences that range from a general feeling of well-being to what can best be described as a spiritual, and sometimes mystical, experience. Here are some stories we have been told:

It was a time of downsizing and the whole company was at a point of low morale and high stress. The manager of the department most obviously targeted for cuts felt a sense of calm about his own future. He knew that he was doing what he was meant to do and was exceptionally good at it. He believed he wouldn't be targeted, but if he was targeted, he was confident that he would soon be able to find the right place somewhere else.

*****

It was another crazy day at the day-care center. Two people had called in sick, an announcement of another funding cut had arrived in the morning mail, a concerned parent was waiting to see her, and a child with paint-covered hands was grabbing at her skirts.

Unexpectedly, a sense of joy welled up inside her. She seldom prayed, but found herself internally singing a prayer of thanksgiving. I must be one of the luckiest people in the world, she thought.

*****

He was on the inside track when he pulled away from the pack. Suddenly his perspective changed. He was no longer aware of the track disappearing under him, but was watching himself as though he were sitting on his own shoulder. He was what race car drivers and athletes refer to as "in zone."

****

After three months of not being able to secure any contracts for her business, she began to panic and started searching for jobs on LinkedIn. With the review of each job post came an unease in the pit of her stomach and the growing awareness that straying from her purpose and her goal to live life on her terms, was not the answer. Instead, she focused her attention on accepting that the road to success is often filled with potholes and unexpected detours, and reconnected with her faith in her abilities and her knowing that the right path to success would present itself to her as long as she remained on purpose. She replaced doubt with faith, and replaced panic with a sense of calm, both of which brought a renewed sense of passion, energy and a new set of clients.

Each of the above describes some of the personal experiences that result from being on purpose. The fulfillment can range from a simple sense of self and well-being, to incredible spontaneous joy accompanied by a sense of appreciation or thanksgiving, to the ultimate—being in zone. Being in zone, or "in flow," as it is sometimes called. The word *flow* itself suggests that achievement happens without struggle. *You are not focused on results, but are completely immersed in the joy of the doing.* Flow comes with no conscious effort when you are working to your purpose.

> *Death is not the greatest loss in life. The greatest loss is what dies inside us while we live.*
>
> Norman Cousins

Purpose has often been relegated to those who dedicate themselves to the betterment of others. Although religions throughout the world and throughout time have taught much about purpose, most who heard about it couldn't see its application in their day-to-day, earning-a-living or climbing-the-ladder existence.

The Sanskrit word for purpose is *dharma.* It translates as "purpose in life." The *Law of Dharma* has three tenets.

- Each of us is here on earth for a specific reason. We each have a mission. We each have a unique talent. When that talent is matched to a need, we can meet that need better than anyone else. Each of us is special.
- Each of us is here to discover our true spiritual self. A popular saying reflects this belief: "I am not a physical being having a spiritual experience, but a spiritual being having a physical experience."
- We are here to serve our fellow human beings. This, expressed in all religions, has often been misinterpreted to mean that we should live an altruistic and sacrificial life. The ancient laws were simply saying that we can and must—if we are going to live fulfilling lives—make a contribution every day in every way, and that we can do this whether we are digging ditches, trading stocks or selling computers. It' a matter of changing our mindset from "What's in it for me?" to "What contribution can I make?"

> *We make a living by what we get. We make a life by what we give.*
>
> Winston Churchill

Being on purpose and being materially rewarded are not mutually exclusive. Quite the opposite. Being on purpose allows us to fulfill our potential, and so obtain whatever rewards are important to us. Most importantly, it means being fully alive and enjoying every minute of the day. Ironically, if we put all our energy into money-making and forget our purpose, we will have to struggle for whatever success we achieve. And we will often achieve less than the monumental effort may deserve. Finally we are beginning to recognize what the poet Bhartrihari expressed hundreds of years ago:

> I thought I was enjoying sense pleasures;
>
> I did not realize they were enjoying me.
>
> I thought I was spending my time;
>
> I did not realize it was spending me.

Psychologist Ernst Becker observed, "People do not so much fear death, but death with insignificance." And Oliver Wendell Holmes is attributed with this poignant description: "Most of us go to our graves with our music still inside us."

Make It Happen: The Indomitable Spirit

"I tried . . . I tried to get a job. I tried to meet the deadline. I tried to start a business. I tried to write a book. I tried to get financing . . ."

Too often "I tried" is used as a get-out-of-jail-free card. As long as we tried, it's okay, isn't it? As long as we tried, we are not responsible. Life is in the hands of fate.

However, whether "I tried " is an excuse or a statement of fact depends, of course, on one's personal definition of *try,* and there are times in most of our lives when we meet insurmountable obstacles.

But people with passion live by Winston Churchill's words: "It's not good enough to say we're doing our best; we must do what has to be done."

, Howard Schultz, Ex- CEO of Starbucks, was turned down by 217 of the 242 investors he talked to when raising venture capital in Starbucks' early days. At what point would *you* have said, "I tried"?

James Dyson didn't give up easily either. As a young inventor in Britain, Dyson relentlessly pursued his vision to create the world's first bagless vacuum cleaner during a time when Hoover was used as a verb almost as much as Google is now. In Dyson's book[9], *Against the Odds,* he recalls being told, "But James, if there were a better kind of vacuum cleaner, Hoover would have invented it." The odds of, as Dyson put it, "an Englishman, who wasn't a qualified engineer, without even a physics O level to his name," and a 'former art student who didn't know a ball-bearing from a Barings Bank,' becoming a significant disruptor to the vacuum cleaner industry by creating a vacuum that would one day become the number one selling vacuum cleaner in Britain (at a price tag significantly higher than a Hoover) and ultimately resulting in worldwide sales of $10 billion by 2002, and then Dyson himself becoming a multimillionaire seemed about as likely as winning the lottery twice in a row. But that is exactly what happened, but only after Dyson had created 5,126 prototypes that failed before his model worked, was turned down by UK and

---

[9] Dyson, James. *Against the Odds.* Orion Publishing Group, 1997

Us distributors and finally launched his own company - years of resilience, hard work and determination.

In 2006 Dyson became *Sir* James Dyson for his contributions to business.

While Dyson-like perseverance and resilience are must-have ingredients for success, it is also critical to know when to accept the fact that your idea isn't going to work. Winners have a keen ability to know when to keep going and when to let go by balancing logic and intuition. We'll discuss tapping one's intuition a little later.

Committing oneself wholeheartedly to success and being able to identify and accept when it is time to let go and move on also requires self-confidence, something that some lucky people seem to be just born with and the rest of us must work hard to develop.

Become Purposeful and Passionate

If you are not living each day with excitement, energy and passion, then you are not fulfilling your life's purpose. We don't mean that each day is filled with rainbows and unicorns and completely devoid of disappointments and challenges, but that you are filled with an energy that propels you forward and a sensation of anticipation for the future that you are creating because you recognize your purpose in life and you are taking action to realize it.

It isn't always easy to get on purpose and to stay there. It takes determination. Being fed up with where you are can definitely fuel that determination. Getting on purpose and discovering what fuels you most in life is a full contact sport and will not occur simply by sitting on the couch day dreaming about your future self; it will take time, soul searching, risk taking, possibly even some embarrassment if you are overly concerned by what others think of you, and it will definitely require stepping outside of your comfort zone in some way shape or form.

> *If you don't fail, it's because you did not risk enough, and if you didn't risk enough, it's because you didn't put your whole self out there.*
>
> Carlos Barrabes

When trying to clarify your purpose, think of what you enjoy *doing—not* what you think you would enjoy *being.* If you think you want to be a Steven Spielberg, the President or an Olympic athlete, ask yourself *why.* Each of these roles has several activities attached to it. Be clear about your own motivation. For example, why Steven Spielberg? Is it that what he does is creative? Do you enjoy film production? Do you enjoy wheeling-and-dealing? Are you attracted to fame and money? Remember, however, that although there is no reason we can't make a lot of money doing what we love, making money or being famous is not a purpose.

Timothy Butler, a highly respected career coach and faculty member at the Harvard Business School, emphasizes that one should think *activity or function,* not role. He encourages people to look for their "deep" interests. He describes core business functions as "not functions, like marketing, sales and finance, but basic activities such as quantitative analysis, perceptual thinking, enterprise control and creative production. If you look at your deep interests and think about how they can be expressed in specific business behaviors, then you will have a good match."[10]

---

[10] *Alan M. Webber. "Is Your Job Your Calling?" Fast Company. March 1998.*

Find Purpose Today

Our lives are made up of millions of "nows." If we lose the "now" in planning for the perfect moment tomorrow—or even worse, waiting for it—we will have wasted our lives. You may not be able to completely fulfill your purpose today, but there are ways to increase your joy in what you are doing now, as well as increase opportunities to make someone else's life better as a result of having connected with you. You can begin immediately to fulfill your purpose in small ways, and that will increase your *joie de vivre* and therefore your energy and chances of success.

Here are some ways to do what you love to do, and to use your unique talents:

- Look around your workplace for ways in which you can make a personal contribution. This may be above and beyond your job description, and your first reaction, if your situation is like most people's today, might be "I don't have time to do this." But we all somehow make time for our priorities. What we really don't have any more time for are activities that are draining or stressful. Doing what you love to do will create energy, not drain it.
- Start with small commitments if you feel overloaded. If you write well, write an article for your in-house or professional journal. Write a blog. If you have a knack for helping people develop, volunteer to be a mentor or buddy for a new employee. If you have presentation skills, volunteer to make your team's next pitch to senior management. By making contributions, you are also strengthening your interconnectedness and raising your profile.

- If you are unable to find a work-related way to use your talents, find a way to express them as a volunteer. Your sense of well-being will be enhanced, and paybacks, direct or indirect, are inevitable.

Do what you can, with what you have, where you are.

Theodore Roosevelt

Apply Your Knowledge

Acquiring knowledge can be like saving money under your mattress. It does nothing for you unless you use it. It is easy to have all the answers. Lots of unsuccessful people know what they should do. The difference between success and failure lies in the doing, not the knowing. The workouts will help you apply your knowledge of the new laws of success, and develop your own winner instinct. The workouts that follow will help you identify ways to begin fulfilling your purpose and finding joy in your work now. They can also be used to help identify new job opportunities.

WORKOUTS FOR DEVELOPING PURPOSE AND PASSION

1: Find Opportunities

1. Put yourself into a relaxed reflective mode.
2. Ask yourself, "What are my unique skills and abilities?"
3. Make a list of those talents you most love to use.
4. Return to a reflective mode.
5. Do a relaxed mental search for opportunities. Remember, opportunities are needs that match your special talents.

6. Screen each potential opportunity by imagining yourself meeting the need identified. After screening each one, select the one that "feels right." This feeling usually combines a sense of belonging with one of anticipation, and excitement or joy. Picture the details; your work environment, the color, the smells, the people around you.

Note: You can continue with workout 2 if you have sufficient time to do it in a leisurely fashion. If not, leave it until tomorrow.

2: Seize the Opportunity

This workout will help you develop strategies for taking advantage of the opportunity you visualized in Workout #1.

1. Put yourself into a reflective mode.
2. Once again visualize the opportunity you felt best about. Picture yourself fulfilling the need you identified.
3. Take a step back in your mind to the "getting the opportunity" stage. Think about who could be instrumental in helping you or what you need to do to move forward. In this step there is a tendency for some people to revert to a mental action mode. Their mind speeds up as does their heart rate. Their muscles tense. If you find this happening, stop and use deep breathing, consciously relax your muscles until you have slowed down again. Then return to searching out ideas for capturing the opportunity. If negative thinking intrudes, filled with all of the reasons you can never achieve what you are visualizing, firmly push it aside, then return to identifying positive strategies.
4. Review every idea in your mind and identify those that feel best.
5. Jot down the ideas you are most enthused about.

6. Develop a mini action plan. Attach a date by which time you will take each step.
7. Commit yourself to your plan.

3: Prepare to Execute Your Plan

1. Put yourself in that relaxed reflective mode. (You should be starting to get the hang of this by now.)
2. Visualize yourself going through each step of your action plan. Picture taking each step perfectly and with ease. If other people are involved picture what you will say to elicit their positive, enthusiastic response.
3. Let yourself experience the feelings as you successfully go through each step—the excitement, anticipation and joy that everything is going so well.
4. Is there any step of your plan that you were unable to achieve in this visualization exercise? Does the plan require modification or do you simply need to work on your level of confidence?
5. Make any revisions to your plan that your mental dry run suggested to you.
6. Mentally relive implementing your plan successfully as often as possible. Then, just do it.

4: Envision Success

For those who want to enrich their lives right now even if they can't immediately begin to execute their plan.

Once you have identified your purpose, your whole life will seem clearer. You will have a primary focus that will act as your rudder. You will begin to reassess how you spend your money and time and with whom.

If you are not able to immediately change gears to fulfill your purpose, start by visualizing how your life will be different once you are working with purpose. The lifestyle we associate with working at what we are meant to do is often very different from the one we are living now. Begin this minute to change your lifestyle to match what you see in your vision; this can improve your quality of life from here on. Often people are in a rut despite a surfeit of good intentions. They tell themselves they will begin to exercise more regularly, read more, go to the theater more often, or have a better work life balance. How often do people say, or more likely think, "When such and such happens then I will ..." When good intentions are not executed it just contributes to the weight of things not being quite what we would like.

Living as though we have achieved what we want to achieve brings success. Use the following steps to begin enriching your present life.

1. Once again find a quiet spot and move into a relaxed, reflective mode.
2. Envision your day-to-day life as it will be when you achieve whatever it is you desire to achieve. Notice your surroundings in detail. What is different from your current surroundings? Perhaps there are bright colors or flowers. Perhaps there are interesting works of art or literature. What are you doing, have just done or are about to do in this scene? Are you reading, playing tennis, scaling a mountain, painting a picture or walking your dog? Who else is in your scene and what is it you are talking about? Enjoy your experience and don't forget to be conscious of what you are feeling.
3. Jot down the pieces of the experience that created the strongest positive emotional response. For example, a feeling of peace, joy or happy anticipation.
4. Select the aspects of your reflective experience that you can replicate now. Perhaps there are touches you can add

to your home environment or office. Perhaps things you have intended to do but haven't gotten around to. You may even develop new friends with interests that are different from those in your present social group. The possibilities are unending.

5. Make your new lifestyle happen.

5: Work for the Joy of It

For those who want to ensure they experience what's really important to them in life and work.

Human beings are seldom fulfilled if their environment does not provide what is important to them. The day-to-day experience is dulled. Sometimes we are not even consciously aware that our current environment is not meeting our fulfillment needs.

Part A

1. List three things that you value.
2. Are these things available to you in your work life?
3. If not, does the absence of these things in your day-to-day work life affect your joy at work, and therefore your success?
4. If the answer to the above question is yes, perhaps you should start looking for other career opportunities.

Part B

If you had trouble identifying the things that are most valuable to you or would like to check that you haven't missed an important one, go through the following list and choose five.

- Having low work stress
- Having a high profile
- Being loyal
- Having power
- Challenging myself intellectually
- Taking risks
- Being competitive
- Learning
- Making money
- Achieving major accomplishments
- Interacting with others
- Serving others
- Feeling needed and appreciated
- Having status
- Having free time
- Being part of a team
- Having job security
- Making my own decisions
- Advancing my career

5. Attach A's and B's to each of the five you choose: A - essential to my feeling good about myself, B – important but not essential.
6. Are your values met in your current work situation?
7. If not, can you change that?
8. If you can't, begin looking for new opportunities.
   Life means having something definite to do- a mission to fulfill- and in the measure in which we avoid setting our life to something, we make it empty. Human life by its very nature has to be dedicated to something.

   Jose Ortega Y Gasset

6: Define Success

Many people define the degree of someone's success by the amount of money earned or the level of their profile. Success to you might be wealth, writing a best-selling novel, building a successful company or being famous. More important to you might be having a healthy and happy family, making a contribution to society, sailing around the world or writing poetry.

Unless we decide what is truly important to us, we can get so busy chasing material success that we miss out on the rest, and may find later that we have aged with regrets rather than a sense of fulfillment.

Here is an exercise that works well for many people:

1. Put yourself in a relaxed reflective mode.
2. Picture yourself at the age of 90, healthy and mentally alert.
3. As that 90-year-old, reflect back on your life. Then complete the sentence, "I wish I had ..." You may come up with one item that is extremely important or a list of several. "I wish I had been able to own a yacht" doesn't usually come to people's minds. Regrets usually relate to relationships that have not been given enough attention, or personal abilities and passions that were not tested and explored. These are the things that are truly essential to our living our life fully, and yet they are so easily set aside when we are too busy attending to the material part of our lives.

Fulfilling our true desire might mean completely changing our life's course. More often, it is simply a matter of not letting our drive for material success become so all-consuming that we dash through our life rather than savoring it.

7: Remember What You Forgot

I know many people who are struggling to find their purpose. They want to find a fulfilling way to earn their living, but, although they are multitalented, they can't quite grasp what they are meant to do. The following is your first step in defining your purpose:

1. List what you enjoy doing. Include everything, including those things you see as being a hobby only such as sports or handicrafts. Identify the parts of your job that give you enjoyment. Also, search through your past work experiences.
2. Highlight those things that give you the greatest sense of fulfillment. You may feel like whistling or singing when doing these things. You may be in a better, more outgoing mood. You'll recognize when you are doing something that in some way fulfills your purpose, because you feel good about yourself.
3. Reflect on your youth and childhood. What did you love to do then? What did you always want to be? These may have been a child's fancy but don't dismiss them too quickly. Was there anything that fascinated you as a child, but was extinguished by well- meaning parents, or simply life's circumstances? Is there an interest that emerged when you were younger that still captures your attention. Jot down any ideas that come to mind. Select three or four that you feel strongly about.
4. One by one picture yourself doing or being involved with each of these in a work environment. Put as much detail in your picture as possible. Imagine the environment, the people around you and your interactions with them. Try to sense how you are feeling as you imagine each scenario.
5. Which image felt most exhilarating? Which made you feel best about yourself?
6. If a forgotten talent or pleasure is your purpose, you will know.
7. If one item does not strongly present itself as your probable purpose, re-read the list you made in steps 1 and 3 and pass the search over to your subconscious; sleep on it. Return to you list briefly in the morning to check whether anything has risen to the top.

Winner's Tip

Your purpose may not emerge immediately. You may not even have it on your list as yet. Read over your list once a day and add to it as more ideas emerge. By thinking about purpose daily, you will condition yourself to be more in tune to potential passions within you and around you.

Law #4

GET INTERCONNECTED

Imagine a powerful computer loaded with the most advanced software, sitting on a desk but not attached to any power source. It is full of potential that will never be realized, unless someone connects it to an energy source. Many people are the same. Possessing capability, replete with potential, but not effectively plugged in to the people around them. Their potential is not realized. One of the most common weaknesses exhibited by people in today's organizations is an inability to connect *powerfully* with others.

At one time, when the world was simpler, we could get by in relative isolation. Today, we need all the help we can get. Consider the following:

- The plum opportunities come through relationships.
- Most successful enterprises are created through partnerships.
- Most important decisions are made and implemented by groups.
- Much of the knowledge and information we need comes from others.

We can no longer single-handedly be all things to all people, or even all things to some people. There is too much knowledge and information to sift through, and by the time we have made inroads, everything has changed. We need a lot of help from our friends.

Take John, for example. He had accepted what looked like a terrific opportunity. He had been hired away from a major brokerage firm to be president of a small, one-hundred-year-old regional firm. His boss handed him a challenging five-year plan: increase broker count by 30 percent, increase the number of branches by 20 percent and increase broker revenues by 30 percent. In the first year, he accomplished more than two-thirds of the plan.

Sound like the beginning of an inevitable success story? Well, the job didn't work out, and Thurston recognized that he had been so focused on meeting his goals that he overlooked the need to connect beyond his immediate team. He didn't develop relationships with people at head office who could let him in on the hidden agendas and unwritten rules. He was several months on the job before he discovered, at a company retreat, that the department heads whose cooperation he had to have were fiercely resisting growth—his mandate.

What lessons can we learn from John's experience?

- Ask more questions of the right people as soon as you start a new job or project.
- Get out of your corner.
- Spend time networking.
- Ask lots of questions.
- Listen more instead of selling.
- Find out about any hidden agendas.

In other words, make sure you are connected with the right people at the right time.

In the discussion of winners in the introduction, we mentioned that winners often have no more skills or knowledge than those who struggle to keep up, nor do they work harder. They are simply more in tune with the requirements of the world and situation in which they are working. Of the 6 New Laws of Success, an ability to be interconnected is most critical. Interconnectedness is the catalyst for, and mainstay of, success.

How well we connect with others depends on our personal style, plus the skills we develop. Increasing our points of contact will only make a difference if we make the connection effectively. We may attend more meetings, chat with more people, embrace social media, volunteer for more task forces or join more networking groups, but unless we connect effectively and make a contribution and present ourselves well, we will squander a great deal of time and gain nothing. In fact, poor connections can *decrease* our power.

And remember, too, that interconnectedness means connecting not only with people, but with ideas and happenings. Our success depends directly on the number and quality—or effectiveness—of these connections.

Know When to Disconnect

Disconnecting with the *wrong people* at the *right time* is as important as connecting with the right people at the right time. This is not to suggest that you use people and then toss them away. The reality is that some people who are not the right fit for you at this time can drain the life from you and your project. There are times when it is important to sever relationships, and to do so quickly.

Keith, for example, had several strong entrepreneurial traits. His systems knowledge, creativity and joy in the process of building an idea into something lucrative have provided him with the fuel to launch innovative businesses. His enthusiasm, not to mention his sincere caring for people around him, drew to him good people who quickly took his belief as their own and became as driven as he. Keith knew how to connect powerfully with people.

But he had one weakness that sometimes got in his way, as it did in one of his ventures: he put total faith in people even when evidence showed they were slipping.

He had built an innovative firm from a fledgling idea to a company proudly listed on the stock exchange. Still passionate about the company and believing in its potential, Keith found himself making a painful decision—to sell his share and leave its leadership and future to others. He knew that things might have been different if his Achilles' heel hadn't acted up on him. He didn't always recognize, or wasn't able to face, the difficult decision when it was time to disconnect. In this case, he gave people too many chances after it was apparent that they were no longer a fit for the company as it grew.

The real turning point came at a critical stage in the company's growth; it had attracted important investment capital. This was its moment of greatest opportunity. Superior judgment and decisive action were essential. "I took my eye off an important ball because I trusted for too long that a key member of my team was making the decisions and taking the actions that were required at that critical time." He wasn't—and although the company continued to progress, it missed the giant leap.

> *Independence? That's middle class blasphemy. We are all dependent on one another, every soul of us on earth.*
>
> George Bernard Shaw

Some relationships are lifelong ones. Many of these benefit both members at a particular place and a particular time. As the situation changes, the fit no longer exists. At that point, the relationship becomes detrimental to at least one party. Knowing when to disconnect, and making the decision to do so, is difficult but important to consider.

"Get It"

We slam doors shut every day, limiting our own possibilities because something strikes us as wrong or unimportant. We might write it off as a "dumb idea." This happens when we cling too tightly to our personal paradigms, our beliefs about what's right and what's wrong.

Every idea or person we cursorily discount without unbiased consideration is a possible opportunity missed. When the waves of change accelerate, it is a common coping mechanism to cling to paradigms as though they were life rafts. People try to hang on to the known—what makes sense to them—to survive. Ironically, they put themselves at greater risk, limiting their success and even threatening their own survival.

Joel Barker, who popularized the paradigm concept, suggested that if something is outside our paradigm, we just don't "get it." A frightening thought. How many opportunities is each of us missing? And how do we know when we are not getting it?

We don't, and therefore we have to develop a personal devil's advocate game through which we constantly challenge our own assumptions. We have to let go of our assumptions, at least for a while, and play the game of assuming the other person or possibility is correct, so that we can openly explore further. Letting go of our paradigms also allows us to access our intuitive sense. Once we are into this free and open space, we may even find empirical evidence, which we earlier ignored, that will "prove" that something we would previously have rejected deserves consideration.

Whether we are searching out opportunities to connect, or having opportunities forced upon us by our work environment through teams and task forces, we are making many more links today than ever before. This linking brings all the potentially valuable outcomes that we have already discussed. At the same time, however, the more frequently we connect with others, the greater the opportunity for miscommunication and, perhaps, negative conflict.

Many people, because of their naturally independent natures or because they haven't been required to work extensively with others, haven't developed the skills needed to make powerful interpersonal connections. Nor can they deal with the negative conflict that can arise when skillfulness and sensitivity are lacking.

Be Strong Enough

Powerful connections are made when we give first. We must be able to give of ourselves, and give of what we have. That may be knowledge, skills or money. It may even be trust—the toughest one of all. Even people who are extremely generous by nature, who may be described as "always ready to do anything to help anyone," have a difficult time truly trusting others. And once trust has been broken—many people attending my workshops have told me—they simply cannot trust again, no matter what the other person does or says to get the relationship, business or personal, back on track.

In a workshop Leslie was leading on teamwork, the topic of trust led to a discussion on why some participants gave money to street people and others didn't. One who didn't give explained why. "Half those guys are faking it. They are on welfare and don't really need the money or else they're just going to spend it on booze or drugs. I'm not going to let anyone take advantage of me."

"If you give someone a gift, and they choose to misuse it, I don't see why you care. You have done something positive. They are the ones losing, not you," another participant responded.

"No way. At least half of those guys are just laughing at you. I'm not giving anybody the chance to do that."

"If someone abused your gift, would they be someone you respected?" Leslie asked the group. Everyone shook their heads no. "Then I have to ask," she went on, "why would you spend any energy worrying about what they think?"

Several people nodded their heads in agreement and understanding. Others simply repeated the original sentiment: "I'll never give anyone the chance to make a fool of me."

When someone is afraid to risk giving, it is a strong sign that their own self-esteem needs some work. Giving trust requires taking risk. Having someone let us down or betray that trust can be painful, particularly if it is someone with whom we believe we have developed a relationship. However, for some people the reaction is more than hurt or disappointment: it is humiliation. That goes back to our perception of being taken advantage of, as though we are somehow less as a result of the other person's misguided behavior. We can only trust when our own self-confidence is strong enough to give the other person entire ownership for their behavior, and not to see it as a reflection of ourselves—that is, "I was stupid to trust him. I should have seen it coming."

We are not suggesting that we should always trust blindly. There are two polarities: complete naiveté and inability to trust. Neither is healthy. Both can be based on lack of self-esteem. As in most things, we need to find a midpoint or balance. But the main question for our purposes is this: "Do I trust readily enough to develop powerful connections?"

Our giving, in general, often reflects our level of confidence. Hesitation to share information or skills is often based on a fear that we will help someone get a leg up, and they might actually get ahead of us. A confident person knows that helping another become stronger does not make them weaker. Successful people do not fear others' strength. They not only generously help others get ahead, but surround themselves with people who are stronger in some ways. If you ever watched the old *Seinfeld* sitcom, you saw this in action. Seinfeld recognized his limited acting abilities and was confident enough to surround himself with strong talent. He didn't worry about how he would look in comparison; he recognized that they would make him look good and enhance his comedic abilities.

To make powerful connections, we must have enough confidence to a) readily connect with as many people as possible, including those we may see as better than ourselves in some way, and b) act with a generosity that widens and strengthens the connection. Healthy self-esteem makes it much easier to develop those connections.

The relationship between communication and confidence is one of those circular issues. The more positive our interactions with others, the better we feel about ourselves; the better we feel about ourselves, the more positive our interactions with others.

Just connecting, however, whether by phone, text, e-mail, social media or in a face-to-face meeting, does not guarantee the kind of communication required for us—or the product we're working on—to benefit. Connecting powerfully requires particular skills. Being able to talk is one of the first and most powerful communication tools that most humans discover. Yet many of us never learn to communicate effectively.

In a discussion on free will, physicist Stephen Hawking said this:

> A society in which the individual feels responsible for his or her actions is more likely to work together and survive to spread its values. Of course, ants work well together. But such a society is static. It cannot respond to unfamiliar challenges or develop new opportunities. A collection of free individuals who share certain aims, however, can collaborate on their common objectives and yet have the flexibility to make innovations. Thus, such a society is more likely to prosper and to spread its system of values.[11]

Or, we might say, "Thus a corporation is more likely to prosper."

In some ways, however, ants are superior to many human work teams. Ants do not think or problem-solve individually or, as Hawking suggests, feel personally responsible for their actions. And yet, despite this tremendous deficiency, ants are capable of amazing accomplishments. Their colonies are wonderful examples of synergy. The whole is definitely greater than the sum of the parts. Although each part (ant) is extremely simple, together the colony performs complex tasks that require integrated behavior. Teamwork is essential. Anyone who has taken time out to watch the activity around an anthill has noted not only their industry, but their coordinated efforts.

Their feats are extraordinary considering individual ants have no creative-thinking or problem-solving ability, as far as science has

---

[11] Stephen Hawking. *Black Holes and Baby Universes.* London: Bantam, 1993.

yet discovered. Nests are simple but functionally designed and built, and underground nests are set up so that lower levels receive enough air. The size of the anthill or mound of dirt on the top regulates the nest's temperature. The more surface area, the warmer the nest. When temperatures drop, ants block entrances with soil; and if conditions become too dry, ants will find water, carrying it back in their mandibles and applying it to the tunnel walls, thereby increasing humidity. As environmental conditions change, colonies adjust by changing the number of workers allocated to various tasks. Ants can create various structures as needed, such as paths between nest and food, or "living bridges" of themselves that stretch across swampy areas in rainforests to accommodate the migration of the colony. Army ants can invade a countryside, sending other creatures scurrying as they transport their queen and her entourage.

The ants' tremendous collective achievements rest on their ability to communicate directly, with no opportunity for miscommunication. They pass messages or cues directly to one another. It is believed most, if not all, cues are passed through antennae contacts, and possibly hormone trails left on the ground. Considering their limited individual brain power, ants' collective behavior far outshines that of humans. Imagine what power we would have if we could communicate more directly!

We humans struggle with a huge collection of communication handicaps that prevent our achieving direct communication. For one thing, we seldom receive information in its pure form. Before it reaches our conscious minds, it has been dissected by our accumulated personal experience, assessed by our cultural values and massaged by our view of the sender.

When a group is at work, the same piece of information is screened and reshaped by each of its members. If there are six team members, the original piece of information becomes six subtle variations of the original. Variations are compounded in group discussion.

We humans are not, however, a completely hopeless lot. We can communicate directly and share pure information if we learn how to dialogue. Imagine the level of synergy we could create if we combined our human level of intelligence with direct communication that sends pure messages. We move toward that state when we enter into dialogue.

Move from Discussion to Dialogue

"Let's discuss it" is usually an invitation to hear another's point of view, develop mutual understanding, and make a decision. The intent and behavior commonly demonstrated in discussions, however, are at odds with one another.

In most discussions, participants, whether two or ten, ensure the process lives up to its roots. Consider related words that come from the same root as the word *discussion—for* example, concussion and percussion—and you have a sense of what happens in most discussions. There is a cacophony of ideas as perspectives clash. Each member owns her personal point of view and sees herself responsible for making sure that others buy that point or, at the very least, understand it. Participants debate at best, and argue at worst. Individual differences that should enhance the process inhibit or destroy it. The potential shared meaning is lost in the noise. Conflict often results.

In contrast, *dialogue* promotes shared understanding instead of individual understanding. From shared understanding emerge new ideas and richer conclusions. Each member leaves a meeting with a common understanding of decisions made, and with a sense of ownership for those decisions. Therefore, not only are decisions that result from the dialogue process superior in quality, but because of the buy-in of all participants, the implementation is also facilitated.

The physicist David Bohm, who spent much of his life explaining dialogue from both philosophical and practical points of view, suggested that the derivation of the word *dialogue,* the Greek word *dialogos* (*logos* meaning "word" and *dia* meaning "through"), means "a stream of meaning flowing among and through us and between us. This will make possible a flow of meaning through the whole group, out of which may emerge some new understanding. It's something new, which may not have been in the starting point at all. It's something creative. *And this shared meaning is the glue that holds people and societies together.*"[12] [emphasis added]

It is essential for us to learn to dialogue, not only with people in our work environment but most importantly with those with whom we are closest. Most of our happiness is based on our ability to connect meaningfully with those whom we care about most. If our personal life is joyful, it provides us with the energy to achieve in our work life. If our personal life is not fulfilling, it is probably sapping our physical, spiritual and intellectual energy. It is doubly challenging, under these circumstances, to achieve the level of success that we desire and deserve. If you recognize the need to strengthen your skill in dialogue, make sure you work on it at home with the same diligence you show at work.

Interactions, at a conscious or subconscious level, are about power. Sometimes when using what are known as *dialogue closers,* an individual can actually feel a surge of power. Uttering a statement of intimidation, such as "You've got to be kidding!" is a conscious or unconscious attempt to control the other person. When we react to

---

[12] David Bohm. On *Dialogue.* New York: Routledge, 1996.

people's ideas or actions with dialogue closers, we not only shut down the interchange, but we deplete the other person's energy. As such, it is self-defeating, since we also obliterate any desire they might have had to link and share with us.

Think about the people closest to you. Do you consistently help them express the best of themselves and bolster their confidence, or do you sometimes make them feel ill at ease and insecure? Such insecurity will make it difficult for individuals to live up to their own, or anyone else's, expectations.

We were once discussing feedback and communication in a workshop we were leading on teamwork. One manager asked if we could use as a case study a problem he was having with his son. Here's what he described: "We have a fourteen-year-old kid and he's driving us crazy. No matter what we ask him to do, he never follows through; he always forgets. We just can't seem to get through to him. Like the other day, we told him over and over again that if he is going somewhere after school, he has to call us or leave a note. So we get home—no message, no Kennie. It was over an hour before he came home, and his mother was getting worried, and I was getting fed up. And that happens all of the time. How can we get through to him?"

"What did you say to him when he got home?" Leslie asked.

"Well, I said something like, 'How many times have we asked you to leave a message? What's wrong with you? Are you deaf?" He looked a little sheepish. "I guess that's a dialogue closer, huh?"

By talking and thinking about his own response to the situation, this manager had begun to answer his own question. He went on. "I felt kind of bad that time because Kennie didn't say much, just went to his room. Later he told us he'd been helping a neighbor who was alone and had fallen off a ladder and broken his leg. He stayed with the neighbor until help arrived."

In fact, this manager was lucky that he did manage to get the whole story. Dialogue closers often prevent people from ever getting the facts. They go through life operating on assumptions, many of them wrong.

Take a moment to replay some of your recent conversations or arguments with the people you care about most. Are you regularly using dialogue-closing statements, or your version of them? If so, you probably have two or three that you use repeatedly. If you can't think of any, ask people you interact with most personally. I can guarantee that they will come up with them immediately.

Simply ignoring people is one form of a dialogue closer. Others include putting hands on your hips, *tich-tiching*, or making statements like "Where are your brains?" "Are you crazy?" "Can't you do anything right?" "Do I have to do everything for you?" "Who do you think you are?"

Closers are often expressed with an inflection, like a question, but they are actually a declaration of what you think of the other person. If the other person has respect or love for you, what you communicate to them paints part of their own picture of themselves.

If you tend to use forms of close dialogue with people you care about, it's likely that you do the same thing in your work world, but by more subtle means. In the following comments on dialogue, I refer to groups and group members, but the same steps apply to fostering dialogue between you and only one other person.

The steps to dialogue are simultaneously quite simple and exceedingly difficult: simple because they are easy to understand, difficult because, for many people, they are not easy to execute. *Dialogue requires that participants put aside egos, personal agendas and assumptions.* Assumptions often include strong opinions of what works and what doesn't, what's right and what's wrong.

Humans spend much of their lives figuring out how the world, or at least their corner of it, works. We have developed our own truths about what the "right" answers are. Our conclusions have come from our personal experiences, fields of learning, and the beliefs that have been transferred to us by those who have played an influential part in our lives, whether parents, teachers or professional role models. It is not easy for many to set those hard-earned truths aside and acknowledge the possibility that someone else's version of reality may be just as "right."

Those who have a high preference for the Convergent dimension in the Personal Task/Process Style Indicator are even more likely to hold their personal and professional beliefs dearly. If you have a high Convergent preference, you will probably recognize—if you are honest with yourself—that you often resist ideas that differ from your own. It is difficult for you to see the other person's point of view. When yours is so clearly "correct," according to your paradigm, you have difficulty seeing past it. Although you may go through the motions of listening to the other person's point of view, you are usually impatient to move things along to the conclusion you believe is obviously correct. Those with a strong Convergent preference must make a conscious effort to develop new behaviors if they hope to dialogue.

> *Faced with the choice of changing one's mind and proving there is no need to do so, almost everyone gets busy on the proof.*
>
> John Kenneth Galbraith

David Bohm cited another problem in attempting to dialogue:

> A further difficulty is you find that very often there is an impulse or pressure, a compulsion almost, to get in there quickly and get your point of view across, particularly if you are one of the "talkers." Even if you are not, you have that pressure, but you are holding back because you're frightened. Therefore, there is no time for people to absorb what has been said, or to ponder it.

Our standard behaviors in most discussions, then, do not lead to dialogue and the resulting powerful connections. On the other hand, as Bohm says, "In dialogue, no one is trying to win."

In traditional discussions, each participant has one responsibility—to get their point across. In dialogue, each person has two responsibilities. The first is to make an active effort to understand others' points of view. The second is to express themselves as effectively as possible to facilitate others' understanding of the point of view they are expressing (but not holding onto for dear life).

Setting aside a personal point of view does not mean sacrificing that point permanently, although you may decide to do so once you have truly listened to others' positions. Setting a point of view aside means just that. If you are a visual thinker, you might picture yourself sitting in a meeting room with others. Each of you is surrounded by your personal beliefs or paradigms developed through years of experience. Many people's paradigms are so strong that they are impenetrable, and ideas that do not coincide with theirs simply bounce off their paradigm shield and never get through to them. People sophisticated in the participatory work world sometimes feign setting aside their paradigms because they know that's what is expected, and they use dialogue openers such as "Tell me more." In reality, however, their paradigms are still firmly in place; they are not able to "hear" the answer.

We must honestly set aside our paradigms if we are going to hear and understand what others are saying. We are not yet giving those paradigms up, but pushing them aside temporarily so other things can get through to us. Once we have understood another's point of view, we may decide to permanently give up or exchange one or two of our paradigms, or we may decide to "put them on" again. If so, it means the value of those paradigms has been confirmed, not just by our own experience but by the group's collective experience.

Once our shields are down, we begin to creative a collective experience.

Dialogue Closers

(a few of thousands)

In response to another's comment:

- "You've got to be kidding!"
- "Don't even talk to me about …"
- "No way!"
- "There is no way anyone is going to tell me…"
- "Well I think …" (completely ignoring the other's input)
- "Where have you been for the past three hours?"

- "That's the very kind of thinking that got us into trouble to begin with."
- "We've tried that …"
- "It doesn't work."

Note: Add to these body language, which speaks louder than words to those who notice it. It can be something as subtle as folded arms or staring at the table rather than looking at the speaker, or as blatant and rude as sighing, groaning and rolling the eyes.

Dialogue Openers

- "I'm not sure I understand where you're coming from."
- "Can you explain a little more?"
- "Let me check and see if I understand your point. I think what you are saying is …"
- "Could you give a couple of examples so I can better understand what you're saying?"
- "I hear what you're saying."
- "It looks as though we are coming from completely different directions. How can we ensure that we do truly understand each other?"

Note: Body language is an important medium here as well. Simply watching the speaker with an open expression, or nodding the head in understanding, encourages continued and open information sharing that leads to dialogue.

Learn the Art of Conflict

> *I cannot give you the formula for success, but I can give you the formula for failure which is, try to please everybody.*
>
> Herbert Bayard Swope

Have you got enough conflict in your life to ensure that you are a winner?

If you agree with everyone all the time, chances are you're walking the safe line of mediocrity. P.T. Barnum's line about not being able to please all of the people all of the time is a truism for successful individuals.

When we ask senior managers what they are looking for in the people around them, one of the most common responses is "independent thinkers." This brings us back to the discussion on risk-taking. Independent thinkers are risk-takers—they know not everyone will agree with them, but because their intuition tells them that in the long run they will be proven "right," they are willing to face disagreement and the conflict that may accompany it.

The doesn't mean pulling on battle fatigues every morning but too little *productive* conflict can result in mediocrity and inhibit your ability to grow.

Increased connectivity is inevitable today through increased teamwork, meetings and partnerships, and will often lead to conflict. However, conflict, when managed and not taken personally, can be beneficial. It creates energy, increases our alertness, forces us to evaluate and often leads to growth. On the other hand, conflict that becomes negative saps energy, increases stress and affects our ability to perform well. Every negative conflict or less-than-positive relation closes a channel through which both participants might have made contributions. You may think, "If he wants to be that way, that's *his* problem." But it's not. It's also *your* problem.

Very few interactions are neutral. We are constantly creating, strengthening, weakening or breaking links. Most of the time we are not even conscious of doing so. Whether we are building up or wearing down connections depends on whether our actions are *link-makers* or *link-breakers.*

Link-breakers cause unproductive conflict. As the number of people we interact with increases, so too does the potential for negative conflict. Conflict is inevitable. Even at home, most of us have at least occasional disagreements with a family member. These are people who probably grew up in the same home as we did, with the same parents and the values they demonstrated. Yet we frequently don't see eye to eye. There can be sibling rivalry, jealously and strongly differing views about how things should be done. Consider, then, the potential for conflict at work, where we interact with people who were raised in different homes, different neighborhoods, perhaps different countries and cultures.

Partnerships, teams and increased participation at every level of every organization mean interactions among people have multiplied greatly in both number and complexity. The opportunity for conflict has grown right alongside them. As a result, being able to effectively prevent and manage conflict is a competency that is increasing in importance. You cannot function effectively today without this skill set.

Nothing is as complex nor as intriguing as conflict. Unresolved conflict can result in wars, murders, lost jobs, destroyed friendships, personal pain, and loss of trust and self-esteem. It lays bare the players' strengths and weaknesses. Yet, conflict also creates an experience through which the characters have the potential to grow. Conflict is an *opportunity.*

Consider the fact that every good play, movie and book is built around conflict and the resulting growth of the characters. When the characters are incapable of growth and therefore meet a sad demise, we see it as a tragedy. Each of us needs to learn how to manage conflict so that we can do the growing without the pain—and certainly without the tragic ending.

Let's be clear about the art of conflict. Anything done artfully is handled masterfully, with skill and beauty. Conflict is no different. Conflict that is handled artfully can result in forward, positive movement. The individuals involved experience growth, and productive outcomes are created that have a beneficial influence on the project or issue at hand.

Does mastering the art of conflict mean that you will always win? No, but you will have the best possible shot at it, and you won't beat yourself up afterwards over what you should have done differently. You will definitely win in the longer term by developing the reputation of knowing what you want and going for it, but doing so with integrity and style. Every time you engage in conflict artfully, you enhance your reputation and build your power to influence.

For more on managing conflict, see Appendix B, How to Develop the Art of Conflict.

WORKOUTS FOR GETTING INTERCONNECTED

See Appendix A: How to Approach the Workouts.

1: Increase Your Connectivity

Note: In completing this workout, refer to the list of Dialogue Closers.

1. List the interactions you have had over the past day or two.

2. Recall each conversation. If they are numerous, choose the most important ones, or those that stand out in your mind. Check the following:
   a. Were you comfortable in the conversation and were you feeling positive about the other person?
      i. If *yes*, you probably did not use dialogue closers, unless you were in a hurry. But did you get as much as you could have from the interaction by encouraging the other person(s) to share information? If so, how did you do it? Did you use dialogue openers? Were you generous in sharing information and opening the communication channels to receive it in return?
      ii. If *no*, you quite possibly used subtle or not-so-subtle dialogue closers.
         - Look for them and jot them down.
         - What might you have lost by shutting down the dialogue?
         - How might you have handled the interaction differently? Jot down dialogue openers that you might have used.
         - Identify your OFIs (opportunities for improvement). Attach commitments to each. Be as specific as possible.

2: Plug In

1. On a large sheet of paper, create a Personal Contacts Map. Put yourself at the center, and scatter around your name the names of everyone with whom you have contact.
2. Identify the people you interact with effectively and frequently. Draw a double line ====== between your name and theirs.
3. Identify those you connect with well, but not frequently enough to be of benefit. Join your name with theirs using a single line ______________.

4. Identify people you do not interact with effectively or comfortably. Draw a broken line - - - - - - between your name and theirs.
5. Now add to your map names of people you seldom interact with, but should. These may be people from whom you can learn, whom you can assist, or who could be influential in helping you. Put a dotted line .... between your name and theirs.
6. Consider people you are connecting with who may be the "wrong" people. (You might want to review the section Know When to Disconnect). These may be people who carry around old baggage and are not ready for the new world.
7. Review your map and decide how you would like it to be redrawn to make new connections.
8. Make plans to do so.

3: How Do You Handle Conflict?

Part A

To what extent does each of the following statements describe you? Use the 1-to-10 rating: 1, not at all, 10, completely.

In conflict situations:

1. I am able to avoid the emotional hook in conflict situations. 1 2 3 4 5 6 7 8 9 10
2. I see conflict situations as interesting challenges to be overcome. 1 2 3 4 5 6 7 8 9 10

3. I make a conscious effort to explore and understand the other person's opinion.	1 2 3 4 5 6 7 8 9 10
4. I am assertive but not aggressive.	1 2 3 4 5 6 7 8 9 10
5. I respond thoughtfully after having given thought to the other person.	1 2 3 4 5 6 7 8 9 10
6. I make every effort to keep communication open.	1 2 3 4 5 6 7 8 9 10
7. I look for the best in the other person.	1 2 3 4 5 6 7 8 9 10
8. I honestly examine my own motives and actions.	1 2 3 4 5 6 7 8 9 10
9. I attack the issue, not the other person.	1 2 3 4 5 6 7 8 9 10
10. I act with integrity.	1 2 3 4 5 6 7 8 9 10
11. I consider the consequences of holding my position.	1 2 3 4 5 6 7 8 9 10
12. I do not criticize my opponent to others.	1 2 3 4 5 6 7 8 9 10
13. I consciously look for creative solutions.	1 2 3 4 5 6 7 8 9 10
14. I hold firmly to positions, that after careful consideration, I still believe to be right.	1 2 3 4 5 6 7 8 9 10
15. I am confident that my behavior earns the respect of my partners-in-conflict and any observers.	1 2 3 4 5 6 7 8 9 10

Total ______

Scoring: A score of 60 or over suggests you are well-schooled in the art of managing conflict. A score of less than 60 suggests you could achieve greater success if you honed your skills.

Part B

If you scored below 60 in the above assessment, examine the statements on which you scored lowest. (*Note*: You are aiming for an 8 or better on each statement.) Choose one of the following approaches:

1. Revisit a past conflict situation. Look at it objectively as a case study. If it was an emotionally draining experience, don't let yourself waste energy by reliving the emotions. Examine each statement in the context of this conflict. Identify specifically what you could have done differently, and then (if you are able to keep yourself emotionally detached) imagine yourself doing it.
2. Examine the statements on which you scored lowest. Develop a personal plan for strengthening each.

Time required: Depending on your earlier score, this could take two or three one-hour sessions.

4: Avoid Link-Breakers

Destructive conflict is often the result of carelessness on the part of one or all participants. They have been negligent in caring for the relationship. Relationships need to be tended or they can easily fray.

Conflict often results when links between people are weakened or broken.

1. Read the information below, which describes the two most common link-breakers: Making Assumptions and Communicating Carelessly.

2. Consider whether you are sometimes guilty of either.
3. If you are, call to mind a specific instance.
4. What could you have done differently? How might a different approach on your part have changed the outcome?

Link-Breaker #1—Making Assumptions

We have all observed or participated in link-breaking scenarios. The most common and destructive link-breaker is making assumptions rather than checking for the facts. Perceptions are assumptions, and are as powerful as facts; people often base their actions and responses on perceptions as though they *were* facts. When we observe a behavior that does not meet our expectations, and if we don't have the information regarding the rationale for that behavior, there is a potential void in our information base. To fill that void, we immediately and confidently create "information" that comfortably fills the void. It is comfortable to us because it fits our first impressions and is in sync with our paradigms. Statements such as "Susan isn't supporting the team" or "Susan is working on a power grab" are perceptions. But as soon as they are slipped in place to fill an information void, they become stored in our minds in the file drawer labeled "Facts." After years of working with people in all types of organizations, I am still amazed by this phenomenon. Why don't intelligent people recognize a void in their information bank to begin with, and then do something to get the required information? Not doing so seems to be a universal human weakness.

We need to recognize when we are making assumptions and need to check for the facts. If you notice a colleague sighing and frowning, for example, you might conclude, "Bob's having a bad day." If you accept that assumption as fact without approaching Bob for verification, it may not lead to serious ramifications. You would, of course, have missed an opportunity to connect with Bob and give him support. But in terms of the organization, and as far as your relationship with Bob goes, the impact would probably be minimal.

However, think about a very different scenario. Imagine your boss does not invite you to what you have heard was an important meeting about the reorganization of the department. You assume, "He's getting me because of the way I blew the big sale last week. I'm obviously on my way down or out."

If you don't check your perception and get the real facts, you could miss the opportunity to solve a problem and at the same time escalate the situation. If you continue to hold your belief that he is angry with you and is looking for ways to "get" you, that belief is likely to become a self-fulfilling prophecy. Your reactions would vary depending on your personal style and coping mechanisms, but here are some probable reactions. You avoid interaction with the boss because you are uncomfortable, and so cut yourself further out of the circle of influence. (He won't have to do it because you will do it for him.) You set up a situation based on which he, in turn, will create his own assumptions. "He knows how badly he blew it last week. He's avoiding me instead of talking with me to try to see what he can learn from his mistakes." When you do interact with him, you will feel some discomfort and will not present yourself as well as you are able.

Your regrettable assumption can be a small but incredibly powerful seed that grows quickly into something huge—with a life of its own. When you hear people ask, "How did this get blown to this proportion?", you can be confident that a seemingly innocuous misperception played an insidious role.

Suppose, instead, you had decided to approach your boss to check out your version of things. "Have you got a minute? I understand from the guys that yesterday's meeting was really important; that you discussed reorganizing the department. I've been worried that I may not have been included because of the way I blew it last week." There are two possible responses:

> "We did end up discussing the department reorganization, but that topic was not originally on the agenda. It came out of another discussion. I didn't think what was originally on the agenda would be of interest to you, and thought you would feel that you could use your time more productively."

> "You're right. I didn't include you because of last week. I felt your actions last week demonstrated that you don't understand how this department is meant to work. I felt therefore that you couldn't make a valuable contribution to the discussion, and that your time would be better spent clearing up last week's problem."

Both responses provide essential information. The first response would set your mind at ease and free you up emotionally to demonstrate the best of yourself. It would also provide a good opener to further discuss any concerns left over from last week's problem. The second response provides less welcome, but clear and important information. You have a better sense of where you stand, the opportunity to clarify your position and to initiate a dialogue about your situation.

Link-Breaker #2—Communicating Carelessly

When we ask people why they don't clarify perceptions and won't communicate openly about issues concerning them, the most common response is that they are afraid they won't handle it well.

Communicating about issues that are important to us can be intimidating. Often we even hesitate to open a dialogue with someone we love. "Will they understand what I'm going to say?" "Will they be receptive?" "Will I only make matters worse?" "Will it result in my revealing too much about my secret fears and weaknesses?"

We could devote a chapter to questions and concerns people share with us about open communication, and particularly about giving feedback. But the biggest and most consistently identified concern is this: "How will the other person react?"

We have reason to be concerned. Much of the feedback I see given and hear about after the fact is careless feedback. It is based on an assumption that their perception is true, and the main message is often delivered in a "you" statement; for example, "You're not being a team player" or "You let everyone down." These statements all communicate that the sender is on the attack.

If you operate on the principle that feedback should make things better, your first step in deciding whether and how to give the feedback is to honestly question your intent. If it is for yourself, or for manipulative purposes, such as "showing them up for what they really are in front of others," you might want to rethink the impulse. You are more likely to be the one remembered unkindly.

Valuable Feedback Criteria

Valuable feedback …

- Is based on the understanding that the purpose of feedback is to make things better.
- Is not given in anger. Take time to cool off.
- Is thoughtful. In this case "thoughtful" does not mean "kind," although that, too, is recommended. Here I mean

thoughtful as in *full of thought*. You should consider (1) your intent, and (2) how best to present the feedback.

- Describes *facts*, including *visible* behaviors (not perceptions).
- Describes the negative impact of the behavior on either yourself (how you feel), the team, the organization, or the deliverables for which you are jointly responsible. By providing this, you have made it clear that this is not a pick-on-someone exercise; the intent is to make things better.
- Gives others the opportunity to express their views on the issue.

In contrast, valuable feedback is given in such a way as to allow the receiver to remain open, so that the problem can be solved. The most important criterion is to ensure that you describe your concern in terms of facts—not in terms of your perceptions, which are your *interpretation of the facts*. If the purpose of feedback is to make things better, then it is obviously important that the person receiving the feedback be open to dialogue. Using perceptions and "you" statements are proven methods for quickly turning potentially positive interactions into negative ones.

5: Check Assumptions

Part A

1. List perceptions you have recently developed about people or situations. Examples could include your perception of a co-worker's performance or a management decision.
2. Analyze each perception, asking yourself, "What am I basing this perception on?" or "How do I know this is true or factual?"
3. Hold yourself to a high standard.

4. Place a checkmark beside the perceptions that are based on insufficient evidence.
5. Decide whether they are indeed important—that is, do they influence your attitude and behavior?
6. If so, how can you better assess these perceptions?

Part B

If you recognize that you are prone to making assumptions, check regularly for them. Ask yourself, "How do I *know* that?"

6: Give Valuable Feedback

1. Consider feedback that you have received in the past and evaluate it against the Valuable Feedback Criteria above.
2. For the situation you were considering above, write a feedback statement that fulfills the criteria.

Note: See also Appendix B, How to Develop the Art of Conflict.

Law #5

TAP YOUR INTUITION

Looking for a new business? Judging by the number of pop-up ads for the service, a psychic hotline looks like a good bet. We are *all* looking for answers, whether in our personal or business lives. The more unpredictable life becomes, the more aware we become of the limitations of the factual information we have at hand.

In earlier times, turning to oracles or sibyls was the norm. Battles were waged and tactics devised, based on their word. Sibyls were usually women put in a trance after consuming a drug or breathing the fumes from a volcanic vent. What they produced were, for the most part, unintelligible rantings that were then interpreted by the priests. It was the interpretation that provided the message. The sibyls were simply triggers for the priests' *intuition.*

Today, more than ever, each of us is inundated with tough decisions. Most of us frequently feel that we could use some outside help. In reality, what we are missing is the *inside help* that each of us has readily available. It's a question of knowing it's there and learning to make use of it. Many of us have hobbled along for years using logic and reason alone—a handicap even in the old world. But today it is impossible to succeed without tapping our intuition—an essential and rich resource within each of us. Reason is no longer enough.

Rational decisions are made by applying logic to information, but we cannot use information created yesterday and logic based on past experience to provide answers for an unknown tomorrow. What may appear to be a quality decision today, based solely on cold fact, is likely to be a mediocre or even poor decision by the time it is implemented.

If there were black belts in decision-making, Colin Powell would wear one[13]. Throughout his many careers as a four-star general, national security advisor to the U.S. president, Secretary of State, and chairman of the Joint Chiefs of Staff during the Gulf War, he has made decisions on a daily basis, the magnitude of which most of us will never face in our lifetime.

Powell has always depended on his intuition and has realized that the older he gets, the more he trusts it. He has consciously developed a decision-making philosophy that balances logic and intuition. He believes that you have to dig up all the information you can—then go with your instincts. He describes the process this way: "I use my intellect to inform my instinct. I then use my instinct to test all this data. 'Hey, instinct, does this sound right? Does it smell right, feel right, fit right?'"

The challenge that Powell, like each of us, faces is time pressure and the inability to ever gather all the information we might like to have. We have to develop an instinct as to when we have enough, and then rely on intuition for the rest.

Timing is essential to any good decision. Powell has developed what he calls a timing formula: $P = 40$ to 70, where P stands for *probability of success*, and the numbers represent the percentage of information required. He does not act if he has only enough information to give him less than a 40 percent chance of being right. Nor does he wait until he has enough facts to be 100 percent right, because by then it is too late.

---

[13] Colin L. Powell. *My American Journey.* New York: Random House, 1995.

He goes with his intuition when he has acquired information in the range of 40 to 70 percent.

Those who are highly logical by nature instinctively try to dismiss intuition because one cannot prove an intuitive answer to be correct by the scientific method. Nor can one prove that it was indeed intuition that led to the best answer.

In our Winner Instinct workshop, we meet some individuals who are not comfortable with the possibility that the best decisions evolve from something other than data. Yet most people have had personal experiences in which their intuition or a "feeling" influenced them in the right direction. A colleague who is very tuned in to her intuitive sense has come to accept its direction without question. One weekend she had planned to go to the country, where she was fixing up an old family farm home to be her retreat and future retirement home. She woke up at four o'clock on Saturday morning and felt that she should get up and leave right away, although there was no logical reason to do so. She did not have to get to the farm at any particular time. Since it was Saturday, there would be no morning rush-hour traffic to think about, and her tired body was loudly voting to stay in bed. But knowing she would regret it if she didn't follow her feeling, she forced herself out of bed and headed for the country.

As she arrived at the farm house, the phone was ringing. It was odd to get a call so early, and she ran across the yard, fumbling for house keys; she reached the phone just as she was certain that it would stop ringing. What answered her out-of-breath "hello" was the weak and distressed voice of an elderly uncle who lived on the adjacent farm. He had been working with gasoline that had ignited, and he had been badly burned. Had she not been there, help would have been some time away. Quite possibly her uncle would not have survived.

Leslie's own intuition has served her well in both business and personal life—when she listened to it. Leslie launched her practice that centered on teamwork way back in the 80's when most organizations were still vertically structured and the label team had little real meaning. Many respected colleagues suggested as tactfully as possible that she was crazy. Teamwork, they said, was a current fad that would disappear in a couple of years, and then she would have to start all over again, find a new product and rebuild her credibility. She understood the logic of what they were saying. One hot human resource management idea after another had arrived, burned brightly for a while, then faded when the next new one surfaced, pressuring organizations that wanted to be on the leading edge to jump on the next bandwagon for fear of being left behind. The assumption was, and too often still is, that if it wasn't a brand-new idea, it probably wasn't any good.

She considered various options, but her intuitive sense kept tugging at her. " It kept telling me that teams would become a top priority for all successful organizations, and that teamwork would be seen as a basic skill required by everyone. I understood the rationale of my colleagues' warnings, but I was certain that the degree to which an organization was able to develop and use highly effective teams would be the key factor in determining that organization's ability to be successful in the new global economy. My intuition took me into a long-term successful business that has provided me with enormous personal satisfaction for over 30 years now."

Make Your Own Luck

Successful people are often seen by others as "lucky." A case in point is Dr. Phil Currie, the respected vertebrate paleontologist whom we met earlier. After spending four summers working at a site looking for dinosaur prints, Currie's team had packed up, left the site and was ready to head home. Some equipment, however, was left behind, and Currie went to retrieve it. As he walked along a river bank, he found a spot that had been uncovered by flash flood activity in the night. Looking down, he found sediment that proved to be 130 million years old, crisscrossed with 170 prints.

On another occasion, "lucky" Currie dropped his camera case. It rolled and came to rest on a rock that turned out to be the skull of a tyrannosaur. "I like to think," he said, "that I'd have found it anyway, but . . ."

Currie, like most successful people, is very aware of the element of luck and a little awed by it. His first response to a question about luck is a logical one:

"You make your own luck. If you are in the wrong place at the right time, it doesn't help. But the reality is that at times you luck into unexpected situations and end up being more successful. Certain people in my field consistently do this. It's as though they have an aura about them. Others are hard pluggers, but don't get the luck. The understanding of luck goes beyond scientific training. It makes you wonder if enthusiasm combined with hard work attracts it."

People who have a sense of purpose and are driven by their passion seem to be luckier than others. Does the energy they exude attract situations? Are they working at a higher intuitive level that connects them with the right events?

Different people have different interpretations of what intuition actually is. It is often described as "knowing directly" or "a sense of knowing", that is, having the answer without having gone through any analytical steps.

Others suggest that intuition is simply knowledge accumulated through experience that is stored at a subconscious level. Without being consciously aware, we may recognize patterns that indicate certain conclusions or "right" directions. For instance, an individual plagued with a health problem may visit doctor after doctor with no success. He finally finds a doctor who has no more clinical information than the earlier doctors, but has a hunch that a particular test should be done, and thus the root of the problem is identified. How did *this* doctor find it? Perhaps by unconsciously noticing a pattern of symptoms similar to symptoms in other patients with the same disease.

It doesn't matter which explanation you are most comfortable with. What is important is that you more consciously tap this resource, which is an amazing gift we've each been handed, if we choose to use it.

It was reported that the remarkable physicist Steven Hawking commented at a White House meeting that he believes we will eventually have to resort to the genetic reengineering of humans in order to keep up with computers. That may be true if we humans continue to operate at our current level. We have been told for years that we are tapping only 2 percent to 10 percent of our brain power. And it's quite possible that the amount we are using is actually decreasing.

In many ways, it seems as though technology is beginning to take on a life of its own and is in a battle against our intellect. As it entertains us and does things for us, we are required to use our minds less and less. With the advent of television and then the internet, people's interest in entertaining themselves has declined. Today's ubiquitous couch potatoes would at one time have done puzzles, played games, conversed more or developed hobbies are now spending hours and hours at a time binge watching entire seasons of television series on Netflix. At an earlier time, radio at least required listeners to participate by creating pictures in their minds.

Computer technologies, from simple calculators to complex problem-solving programs, allow us to set aside math and other basic problem-solving and language skills. Can you imagine sending an email without spell check? The rationale supporting this direction? Instead of using our energy to perform calculations, we can be focusing on applying the outcomes and doing more sophisticated problem-solving. In theory this may make sense, but there are two concerns. We know that anything we don't use, we lose. If indeed the abilities lost are replaced by higher level abilities, perhaps there is an argument. But we regularly witness the weakening of people's basic skills, and don't see a remarkable increase in the quality of higher level replacements.

Members of today's society have an increased awareness of health issues and yearn for toned bodies. Gyms are full of people bench-pressing, bike-riding and body-sculpting. Joggers weave in and out of pedestrian traffic and a record number of people are now cycling to work. We are aware of the importance of exercising our skeletal muscles but don't recognize that it is also important to regularly stretch the brain. Stephen Hawking, in his book *Black Holes and Baby Universes,* states that the human brain contains about a hundred million billion particles. It shouldn't be difficult to increase our brain power. We certainly have plenty to work with.

If we can learn to use what brain power we have more effectively and learn to tap our intuition, we can move to a much higher level *without* genetic reengineering. As civilized beings, we have suppressed a great deal of our intuition. The more we are taught about what's right and what's wrong, and what works and what doesn't, the more we are likely to ignore our intuition. The greater the focus on reason in the society within which we live, the less likely we are to *hear* our intuition. As humans, we long ago recognized the need for order and rules if people were to live and work effectively together. We set out to become civilized, rational beings—all for very good reason, but without recognizing that we were losing the intuitive sense that had long protected us and prevented us from becoming extinct. Now it is our intuitive capacity that is all but extinct.

Gavin De Becker, in his book *The Gift of Fear*[14], claims that in North America we are conditioned to ignore our visceral, intuitive promptings of fear and danger in favor of denial and detached logic.

---

[14] De Becker, Gavin. *The Gift of Fear: And other Survival Signals that Protect Us from Violence.* Boston, Mass.: Little, Brown, 1997.

He presents the scenario of a woman alone in an underground parking lot, approached by an apparently pleasant man offering to help. The woman probably intuits *danger . . . enemy.* But how does she respond? *Politely,* because most people have been brought up to be polite. We have been brought up to go out of our way not to offend. And so the woman smiles and says, "Oh, thanks, no, really I'm fine. Thanks for your offer, but I can manage." She sends the predator the message *easy prey.* Had she been responding according to her intuition, she would have sternly and abruptly responded, "No, I don't need your help."

Our learned behaviors often stifle our intuition altogether or tell us to ignore it when it does attempt to surface. Perhaps it is because our conditioning in this rational world so frequently stifles intuition that brilliant ideas often emerge when we are not actively searching for an answer. Answers often arrive full-blown when we are not wearing our logic-oriented critiquing hats. That's why many people find sleep or rest conducive to intuitive problem-solving and keep pen and paper beside their beds.

Voltaire is purported to have frequently spent fourteen to sixteen hours in bed, calling his secretary when an idea came to him that required recording.

Banting's formula for insulin came to him in the middle of the night. He had been working in the evening, preparing a lecture on diabetes, reviewing cases and experiments that had been performed on dogs but that had proven to be of little use. He worked late, went to bed and woke suddenly at two o'clock with a formula in three sentences in his mind. *Tie off the pancreatic duct of the dog. Wait six to eight weeks for degeneration. Remove residue and extract.*

Intuition functions at its best when we are not imposing too many logical thoughts or anxieties on it. A relaxed state seems to increase access to nonlinear processes. Often intuitive ideas come unbeckoned. So what we need to do is exercise our intuition so that we can use it more on demand.

Laura Day, who describes herself as an intuitive, suggests one method.[15] She describes intuition as usually coming to us in symbols. She explains that intuition proceeds in two steps.

1. response to a question: nonlinear
2. interpretation of the response: both linear and nonlinear

Step 2 includes interpreting the symbols and piecing them together. According to Day, intuition activates in response to the questions we consciously or unconsciously ask.

Some people—such as Day, who has been aware of and using her natural talent since she was a little girl—are naturally in tune with their intuition, just as people who are athletic by nature are more in tune with their bodies. But all of us can greatly increase our intuitive abilities if we choose to do so.

Several factors enhance our access to intuitive knowledge. By simply being aware of these factors and putting them in play, we can become much more "in tune." Remember, they may not all be in play in every situation.

- **Reflection** While we are immersed in data, the mind is hard at work. When we are in a heads-down mode, we are unlikely to notice the quiet intuitive messages. To reflect is to let the mind relax. It may play lightly with some of the information, or it may set it aside for the moment. The mind is not hanging on to the problem and the information surrounding it, but letting it go.
- **Attitude** When one is working with a sense of joy, excitement, anticipation or enthusiasm, intuition readily offers ideas and solutions. On the other hand, when we are tense and

[15] Laura Day. *Practical Intuition.* New York: Random House (Villard Books), 1996

negative, and when what we are doing is drudgery, we are less likely to be tuned in to our intuition. It is as though the channel through which intuition is accessed is shut down. Perhaps this is why people who are "on purpose" are often perceived to be lucky. Their joy in their work allows them to be tuned in to information others will not receive.

- **Setting the problem aside**. Many of us automatically use this technique. "Let me sleep on it" is a common response when a decision is requested. People who, like Bertrand Russell, consciously turn tasks over to their intuition recommend thinking hard about the issue and all aspects of it, and then forgetting about it. The solution most often arises when we are doing something else. The dilemma for many is that if the issue is a serious one, they have *difficulty* letting go of it. They may be on the golf course or at a party, but part of their mind is worrying over the problem. Setting the problem aside means training our minds to let go, at least for a while.

Becoming intuitive simply means learning to look *within* to solve problems *without.* Some people are by nature better tuned to their intuitive selves; some eventually learn to listen to their intuition; the rest go through life not realizing the advantage those with intuitive power have over them.

Risky Business

We have, for the most part, been brought up in a rational world. Something either makes sense against our personal measuring stick—or it doesn't. When we use our intuition, we are depending on an idea that may not be substantiated by facts and figures. Sometimes we go by a feeling or a hunch. Sometimes a rationale emerges to support the intuition, but not always. Often we have a sense of what is right. It may be the right cover for a book, an idea for an article or a solution to a business problem. When asked why, there is no rational explanation; it just feels right. That response is not in the least bit comforting to highly logical people.

Most of us, if we pause to reflect, will recognize that we have frequently made decisions that ignored logic or had only a little logic to support them. We filled in the blanks with our "feelings" because we had to, or because we chose to rely on something other than logic—the job that "felt" right, although you couldn't be sure until you'd tried it out; the mate you chose, even though certain facts (as well as friends) said "no way"; your move to a different city, where a hundred unknown factors would interact to determine your happiness there. Sometimes you were tuned in to intuition, and you worked or lived happily ever after; at other times, what you were feeling was wishful thinking masquerading as intuition. With practice, you can pick out the fraudulent feelings.

Out of necessity, we are all making more decisions these days based on visceral messages. We often have to make decisions too quickly to be able to collect all the pertinent information. All the information that we would like to have simply may not exist, as no one has done before many of the things we need to do today. Pioneers don't have road maps. And we are so inundated with information that we can't possibly use all of it in our decision-making. We may say that we are going with what we have and "a wish and a prayer" or "our best guess," but in these cases we are really relying on our intuition. Sometimes it serves us well; other times, because of lack of use, we don't hear it, or logic overrules the idea it presents.

You can learn to strengthen your intuition so that it is louder and you can't miss hearing it. You can develop a clearer sense of what your intuition feels like so that you can better separate it from wishful thinking. But until we hone our intuition and become as comfortable with it as we are with logic, there will be an element of risk attached to using it. And that means risk-taking, always part of a rich life, is now an essential ingredient to success.

Though the world today is a field of opportunities, there are traps to be avoided. So harvesting the opportunities requires some risk-taking. But the biggest danger is that those of us who are not risk-takers become so focused on looking for the traps that we completely miss the possibilities. If we wait until every trap is sprung, it will be too late; the opportunities will already be plucked by those who were willing to take the chance.

Using our intuition requires a leap of faith. As we learn to tune in to our intuition more clearly, the leap becomes shorter. But since we can't *prove* the move to be right until we follow it, there is always going to be a degree of risk.

Winners know when to take risks. They believe in themselves, and that includes believing in their intuition.

> *Life is either a daring adventure or nothing at all.*
>
> Helen Keller

There is a documentary on the cliff divers in Acapulco. The camera takes a close-up shot of a diver. His face is tense. There is a hint of fear. Just as the diver leaves the cliff, the cameras pan to the bottom, showing what the diver sees as he descends. Directly below him, where he will land, is sheer rock. Then, a huge wave of water rushes in as he descends to the bottom. He hits the water and quickly surfaces to swim to shore before the water rushes out again. If the diver had waited until the water was in before he dove, it would have washed back out, leaving bare rock by the time he reached the bottom. A few seconds' hesitation would have turned a good dive into a deadly one.

Those who have winner instinct are able to sense the right moment, and have the courage to seize it. As the pace of change continues to accelerate, the approach to those moments is shorter, and so is the length of time the "right" circumstances are within our reach. "He who hesitates is lost" is a cliché that holds more truth today than ever before.

Some people are risk-takers to the point of recklessness; others are cautious to the point of immobilization. Fear of the unknown, lack of confidence, fear of being wrong or fear of failing can prevent people from even trying. A young woman who attended one of or seminars described her extreme fear of risk-taking, caused, she believed, by an extreme lack of confidence. She had applied for a job that she very much wanted. She was told that she would be notified within a week as to whether she was chosen for the position. She agonized every day. She was sure that she had presented herself poorly in the interview and that the call, if it came at all, would be to say "Thanks, but no thanks."

"I just couldn't take the risk of failure," she admitted. "Even the thought of being turned down was agony. I couldn't bear to have to deal with the real thing. So the day before they were to call me, I called the woman who interviewed me and told her that I was very sorry but my plans had changed and I had to withdraw my application. 'I'm so sorry,' she told me. 'We wanted to offer you the job." This is an extreme example, but many people tragically never fulfill their potential or their dreams because they are afraid to risk.

We have worked with people who have turned down promotions or opportunities to publish articles for fear of not being able to meet expectations. Some turn down transfers from less-than-happy situations because to them a very imperfect known is better than an unknown—even though the latter might be much, much better.

And then there are people who aren't afraid but seem unable to mobilize themselves. They are enveloped by lethargy. They manage to meet the requirements of the status quo but can't muster the focused energy required to commit themselves to taking a risk.

There is no growth in the comfort zone. If we don't risk, we will not grow. It is impossible for us as living beings to be in a constant state. If we are not growing, we are dying.

In which direction are you moving today?

WORKOUTS FOR TAPPING YOUR INTUITION

See Appendix A: How to Approach the Workouts.

1: Get to Know Your Intuitive Self

Part A

1. Think about whether you actively use your intuition—that is, do you call upon it when you need extra help?
2. If so, is the information you receive clear and helpful?

If you responded yes to both questions, you may not need the intuition workouts that follow and may choose to move on to the next law: Promote Yourself.

If you responded no, go to Part B.

Part B

1. Can you identify an instant when you acted successfully on your intuition?
2. If yes, think about how the intuition came to you. What signals did it use to get your attention? Did a physical sensation alert you? Was it a feeling? If so, how would you describe it?

   If you find it difficult to respond to this question, put yourself in a relaxed reflective mode. Try to visualize when the intuitive thought came to you and how it felt.

3. Can you identify an instance when you acted on your instinct and the results were *not* positive?
   i. Did the feeling you acted on differ from what you experienced when you were successful?
   ii. Could you have been influenced by wishful thinking because you particularly wanted or needed a specific outcome?

Jot down any differences you can identify between intuitive signals that drew your attention to valid thoughts or insights (hits), and signals that drew your attention to invalid ideas (misses).

2: What's Your Gut Feeling?

Part A

1. Keep an Intuition Diary for at least the next week. Jot down each time you have an intuitive/gut feeling about something. Ideas and people's names that pop into your head are intuition at work. You may, for example, suddenly

feel the need to call home or to call a client you haven't spoken to in ages.

2. Also jot down any feeling or physical sensation that accompanied the idea.
3. Record whether you responded to it, and what the outcome was.

Part B

1. Review your Intuition Diary. Is there any similarity in the hit signals and the miss signals?
2. Make note of them. For example, for me the hit signals keep nagging at me if I try to ignore them. If you can't distinguish between them yet, continue with your diary.

Part C

1. For the next week continue your diary, this time responding only to the kind of intuitive signals that last week were hits.
2. Assess your score.
3. If it is not great, go back to Part A again. Remember, a perfect score is unlikely. Expect a few misses. Focus on improving your number of hits. Every time you use intuition well, you are gaining an edge.

3: Just Ask

Our intuition responds to specific questions. The question may be as simple as "Where will I find a parking space?" or may be about more important aspects of our lives, ranging from "Who can help me find the right job?" to "How much should we offer for that house?"

The following techniques will help you tune in to your intuition. As you practice, you will find that your intuition will seem to become stronger. But, actually, it is your ability to recognize and understand the messages your intuition is sending that is growing. Your intuition is already powerful; your skill in using it may not be.

A. Formulate a question, the answer to which would benefit you either in your personal or business life.
   Ensure that your question is specific. For example, if you are considering taking a job with ABCTech, a question such as "Is ABCTech a good company?" is not specific enough. It may be a good company, but not the best place for you to be working. A better question might be, "Is MABCTech a good choice for me as a place of employment?" Even more specific, and better still, would be identifying what you want from the job and formulating a question as to whether ABCTech will meet those needs. But only one need per question. Also, compound questions such as "Should I buy XYZ stock and keep it for five years?" just confuse things. The answer to "Should I buy …" might be yes, but the time frame might be wrong.

A. Once you have formulated a specific, clear and simple question, do the following:

   1. Move into a relaxed reflective mode.
   2. State the question and let it go.
   3. Let your mind wander for a few minutes. Note any strong impressions or images that float through your mind. They may not be obviously linked to your question.
   4. Jot them down in your notebook.
   5. Reflect on the impressions and images that you have jotted down. Do they take you toward a possible answer?
   6. If not, restate the question once more and be aware of any strong ideas or feelings that come to you.

4: Intuition on Call

1. Think hard about a problem or situation that you would like to be better able to handle. Formulate the specific question you need answered. Look at it from every angle. Tear it apart. Ask others' opinions, if appropriate. Review all information pertaining to it. Use every ounce of your logical mind to wrestle with it.
2. Then set it aside—completely! Don't let it nag at the corner of your mind. Don't carry it on shoulders that are hunched up to your earlobes. If you have difficulty setting it aside, distract yourself: play tennis, brush up on your Latin (that should do it) or play chess.
3. Leave it, if time permits, for at least a day. A solution will probably pop into your head when you are not thinking about it.
4. If this doesn't happen, return to the problem, but in a relaxed state of mind. (Do deep-breathing exercises before returning to it, if necessary). A solution is likely to emerge.

5: Problem-Solve at Work

1. Before moving into a problem-solving session, either solo or with others, take time to put yourself in a relaxed reflective mode.
2. Consider the problem in a detached manner, so that you are looking at it rather than immersing yourself in it.
3. Jot down ideas and solutions that emerge.
4. Move into the problem-solving phase. Try to stay relaxed. Assess the ideas and solutions that you jotted down during your reflective time.
5. Select a solution.
6. Take a break. If you are in a group, move away from the meeting table to reflect alone on the chosen solution. Does it "feel" right? If so, move ahead. If not, think again.

Law #6

PROMOTE YOURSELF

We are all *products.* Some people recognize this more clearly than others, and some are more creative and take more risks in packaging themselves.

Nigel was a man facing a career challenge. He felt he was meant to write, and decided that copywriting was the career for him. However, advertising is a popular industry, and competition is high for whatever opportunities exist. Ryce had taken a degree in International Development Studies and had no copywriting experience or training. "Go back to school" was the advice he received most often. Ryce, however, saw the solution to his dilemma somewhere else—in jars of pickles. He purchased several, removed the labels and replaced them with one on the front that carried his name and mini-resume, and another on the back that listed his qualities.

Ingredients: 90% water, creativity, dedication, energy, ingenuity, friendly disposition, adaptability, communication skills and vinegar.

He then had the jars delivered to advertising firms. Even in the advertising business, sending out pickle jars as a resume was risky. In one follow-up call, he was quickly dismissed by someone who told him, "I hate pickles." However, someone else was impressed, and Nigel got the entry he was looking for.

The pickle jar idea would not work in all industries. But the point is that in every field, a job-hunter has only a few minutes to get attention and communicate their ability.

Most of us recognize the need to sell ourselves when we are job-hunting or looking for new business, but many of us forget that self-promotion is just as important once we have been hired or have secured the contract we're after. And this applies even if we have been with the same company for many years. Indeed, selling ourselves at that point in our careers may be even more important, because the longer one's years of service, the greater the chance of one's being taken for granted and overlooked for key positions and promotions.

As well as working hard and being good at what they do, most people who excel have learned to flaunt what they have to offer, albeit with taste. We frequently hear people complain when someone else has received a promotion or a sought-after assignment. There's resentment in the voices of people who say, "I could have done that job!" Perhaps they could have, but the managers making the decision either didn't know it, or, if they did, they were more impressed by the employee who did a better job of selling himself. A superior product can be sitting on a store shelf, but if everyone walks right by it, its quality is worthless.

If you were a product, how would you be perceived? There are three requirements critical to a product's success:

- A primary product of high quality. The primary product is the naked product without the packaging. It is what's being offered that will meet a customer's need.
- A strong brand image or persona that is conveyed widely, but in a targeted fashion through marketing. Marketing includes advertising and packaging. A strong image requires differentiating what you are offering from what the competition is offering.
- A clear target market.

If any of these factors does not receive sufficient attention, the product, no matter how great its potential, will go unnoticed and quickly disappear from the marketplace.

Know Your Primary Product

Compared to people who need to sell themselves, it's easier for Kellogg's or Apple to be clear about their primary product, and for their customers to easily identify with their goods. Corn flakes, computers and iPhones are concrete products. Your product consists of knowledge and skills, and is not as easily recognized. Is it easy for people to match your product to a need? They first have to be clear about what your product is, and before that can happen you must be clear about what you have to offer.

Stop reading for a moment and think of the strongest asset that you have to offer. If you identified it immediately, that's good news. If you hesitated or are still pondering, you are not ready to start marketing yourself. If you are not clear about what you have and want to offer, how can anyone else know your strengths? And more importantly, how can you and your strengths come to others' minds when a need you can fill appears? (And those opportunities are appearing constantly.)

I often receive calls from people looking for advice about establishing themselves as independent consultants, or offering their services on a contract basis. They are frequently interesting people with eclectic skills and ideas and an entrepreneurial spirit. Their weakness is often that they lack focus. They are good at many diverse things and can see all as potential money-makers.

When we talk, I emphasize the need for them to identify their greatest strength and love (being able to do something well, but not being inspired by doing it will bring only short-term success), and to focus on that strength in order to create an identity. Of course, that is common sense, and they nod their heads. Many, however, aren't able to choose among their strengths, or don't have the discipline to focus (a challenge, since by nature entrepreneurs thrive on variety). They expend an enormous amount of scattered energy—and money—before they accept the need to focus and eventually regroup. Many who have fabulous ideas and great potential never do manage to focus, and they waste their dream of success.

Now, these are people who want to make their living selling their services. The incentive is very high for them to be clear about exactly what they have to offer. And yet many never clarify that focus. Imagine, then, how many people *inside* organizations lack focus because they may not have such a self-evident incentive.

The basics for ensuring that you have a highly competitive product are as follows:

1. Choose something you do very well and enjoy doing.
2. Once you have identified your product, do a quality check. Could you offer your product—whether it is selling, auditing, designing Web sites or grooming dogs—as "the best on the market"? If you are serious about your quality, ask your customers and colleagues what they think. You

might ask simply, "What can I do to improve what I do?" If you ask the general question, "What do you think of my (skills or knowledge)?" there is likely to be a vague answer, usually in the affirmative. "You're doing okay," or "You're doing great." Even if you actually are "doing great," you want to find out how you can be even better.

3. Put in place whatever steps are needed to ensure that your product is top of the line.
4. Put a personal audit system in place to remind you to evaluate your performance regularly to ensure continuous improvement. Remember, yesterday's success may count for little tomorrow.

Whether you plan to experience greater success (notice I say "plan to," not "hope to") inside your current organization, inside another organization, or as an entrepreneur who will create their own company, being clear about what you have to offer is essential.

Create a Successful Image

The image for a product is developed through marketing and word of mouth. Your image is created through an accumulation of everything you do and say, every day. Are you seen as a plus person—someone people feel good about in every way, or a minus person—someone people may have some reservations about? How much credibility do you have?

Your image or credibility includes the quality of your product, as we discussed above, and how it is perceived. Your image also includes how you are perceived personally. How do you rate on each of these image factors? Do you believe others see you as:

- highly competent at what you do?
- someone who gets a job done (no excuses)?

- approachable?
- enthusiastic?
- someone who pulls their weight?
- someone who follows through on commitments?
- someone who can be trusted?
- someone who works for the good of the whole (either team or organization) rather than building a personal empire?

Did you answer "Definitely!" when you read each of the statements? Are you convinced that anyone who has worked with you would answer "Definitely!" to each of the statements?

Just as checking with others can enhance the quality of your primary product, checking with others can do the same for your image. You might ask co-workers to rate you on each of the statements, perhaps using a 1-to-4 scale (1-low, 4-high). For any statement not rated a 4, explore with them why they selected the rating they did, and, of course, what you could do differently.

Prevent Negative Impressions

Too often valuable employees, with much to offer, may be left sitting on the bench because of something that happened some time ago, even years ago. A stigma still remains. It doesn't matter whether the perceived image is based on fact—it is as powerful as fact. Once it has been decided that a person has a certain trait, critics will inevitably note any action or comment that confirms their belief. They may even misinterpret something the individual does because the misinterpretation better fits the negative image.

Once an inferior label has been firmly affixed, it is difficult to shake it loose. After struggling against the image for some time, an individual often gives up and withdraws within the organization, or else leaves the organization altogether. In the first instance, a person's potential is wasted and left to a joyless work life. In both, the organization misses out on the contribution the individual could be making.

Since turning negative images around is so difficult, the ideal strategy is to prevent them from being created. When someone misunderstands something that you've done or said, it can be tempting to say, "To heck with them. If that's what they want to think, let them think it." The new world is not a place to let pride get in the way. It's essential that we maintain a strong, positive image. If you allow negative impressions to stand, you are handing other people—who can meet the same needs as you—an advantage. They could have lesser skills than you, but if they have a better image, they are likely to be the first choice.

Bill worked as a member of a web design team. He was acknowledged as being highly creative, and had even won awards for his work. When a new large contract came in from a high-profile multinational corporation, Bill assumed that he would be the lead designer on the project. However, if team members were asked to describe Bill, they would probably say, "Talented, not dependable and not always trustworthy." (Imagine that on a product label.) He was considered not dependable because he often didn't follow through on time commitments he made to team members. There was a lack of trust among his colleagues because, although he always espoused the good of the team, it seemed that anything he strongly advocated for would eventually be revealed as being good for Bill.

The coveted project was one that demanded a team effort. Bill did not get the plum role; in fact, he wasn't even on the team. He was given a couple of smaller, low-profile projects that he could work on independently.

Karen, who won the role, had skills that were not quite as polished as Bill's, but she had excellent team skills, and as soon as her appointment was announced, people were lined up to be on the team. Management knew that for this project a synergistic team was much more important than a star. They were confident that the synergy would result in a high-quality product and a smoothly running project.

Winners have an aura of successful energy around them. You'll never find them in the negative-talk group. During tough organizational times employees often have plenty to complain and worry about, and for some, negative talk becomes a habit. It seems they can't go for coffee without pulling out negative talk. It's as addictive as smoking. You've probably noticed that negative talkers seem to gravitate to one another. Pretty soon, most of their time is spent talking derogatorily about others who have been promoted or given the best assignments or senior management's poor decisions. The negative talkers become a group of losers in spite of their ability.

If you can identify with this scenario, break the negative habit immediately and look for opportunities to spend time with the positive people in your company or your circle of friends. Break away—and stay away—from negative thinkers. No organization has spare energy to expend in order to drag negative people along with it. They will be cut loose. Most importantly, their negativity can sap your own positivity.

Be Visible

Being visible does not mean bragging about one's accomplishments, although as much as most people don't like braggarts, bragging sometimes seems to work. But being visible does mean that you must talk about your accomplishments. If you have a high Independent score, that may not come naturally to you. (See the Personal Task/Process Style Indicator.) You are probably the one who draws others out in discussions to talk about their successes—and everyone leaves knowing nothing about what you have been up to. Learning to chat casually about yourself is important to your success.

> *Doing business without advertising is like winking at a girl in the dark. You know what you are doing, but nobody else does.*
>
> Stewart Henderson Britt

It can mean attending and participating in meetings and volunteering to take on projects that will raise your profile. It can mean maintaining your position and the visibility that goes with it by expecting fairness, by expressing concerns and being assertive about what you believe is fair, and by asking for what you believe you deserve. If people have mistakenly underestimated our ability, we have to remind them of our value and assertively (not aggressively) let them know that we expect fairness. If we are silent, what can they assume but that their perception is right?

Package Yourself

Good packaging gets attention and communicates the quality and positioning of the product. This is communication, not through the fine print on the label, but through color, shape and graphics. A quick glance communicates whether it is low- or high-end, aimed at the mature or youth market, conservative or trendy.

What does your packaging tell people about you? Packaging communicates who you are, even if people don't know you. It is said that in interviews we have three minutes to sell ourselves. The interviewer's mind is, for the most part, made up, influenced indelibly by the first impression—our package.

Packaging is just as important on a daily basis. We are continuously sending messages about who we are and what we have to offer to everyone with whom we interact or even pass in the hall, or sit beside in the cafeteria or in a meeting. Packaging includes how you look, speak, walk and present yourself. It includes whether you have energy in your step, a sparkle in your eye, an easy smile and warm handshake, and appropriate dress. (By appropriate, I mean clothes that help you send whatever message you want to send.) Packaging communicates confidence or lack thereof, stress or well-being, joy or sadness, a caring or indifferent attitude, energy or lethargy. You are revealing who you are every moment, even when you are saying little or nothing.

Be conscious of who and what you project. Often people get lazy, or let themselves slip to the lowest common denominator. That does not mean one has to calculate and orchestrate everything they do for effect. Phony packaging never works. Don't try to package yourself as someone else, or as something you're not. Be authentic, but ensure your packaging is projecting the best of yourself.

And packaging goes far beyond how you dress. Although how you dress does communicate something about you, other aspects of your packaging can convey who you are and your uniqueness even more powerfully.

Remember, your packaging includes the following:

- what you do
- what you say
- how you look
- how you act
- anything you produce that is peripheral to your product, such as correspondence, e-mails, blogs, tweets or anything else on social media and resumes.

Differentiate Yourself

What differentiates us is not just what we do; in fact, that may not differentiate us at all—many others may do the same thing. Who we are much more clearly defines our identity. Hundreds of others may be able to do what you do, but no one else can do it quite like you can. You may be more articulate, have a better sense of humor, work harder, have greater commitment, and be more creative.

We are in awe of unique jewels or works of art. People pay millions for them. Yet none compare to your own uniqueness. Thousands of variables come together to make you who you are. Your characteristics that are praised, together with your peccadilloes, make you special. And within that potpourri of traits are those characteristics that can differentiate you, and so greatly increase your success potential. That is, if anyone knows about them. Showcase them with class.

We also differentiate ourselves by what we can do that is in addition to our primary product, that complements and enhances it. Two skill sets in particular are in demand, no matter what your profession or your role. An ability to create synergy and to influence others puts their owners effectively in the play in today's flat and highly interconnected world of work and business. If you can add these to a strong primary product image, and package these skills so that you will be differentiated, you will bring added value to whatever assignment you undertake. Move quickly to develop these while they still give you the edge. They are already becoming basic requirements in many corporate environments. Soon they will not provide an edge, but their absence will be a disadvantage.

Create Synergy

Synergy gives you a strong edge. It provides the energy you require to get beyond mediocrity. Synergy means interacting with others in such a way that the whole becomes greater than the sum of the parts. It means that people are working as a highly effective team. It may be a team of two, or a team of many. Synergy can be achieved whenever people come together to fulfill a shared purpose. People interacting powerfully together produce much more than the sum of each of those individuals' outputs, had they been working independently.

The greatest waste today is the dissipated energy that results from people working in groups with no synergy. Each member may be giving 110 percent, but if the individual efforts are not coordinated or woven together smoothly and creatively toward a shared outcome, the results are frustratingly inadequate. The less effective the group effort, the greater the tendency of individuals to go in their own direction and look after their own interests. And so the group performance quickly spirals downward into self-destruct mode. You can't afford to waste your time, energy and talent working in such a group.

If you can create synergy, you can be much-in-demand. Although most companies invest a great deal of money, time and energy bringing about change, processes too frequently do not produce the expected results. The change that takes place is too often only physical change. Turning water into ice is physical change. The ice may feel and look different, but in reality it is still the same old stuff—water. What is needed is chemical change. In chemical change, elements interact in such a way that the elements themselves change and create something that does not have only one or two different properties from the original, but is actually a new substance. Chemical change is substantive change.

In the work world, the elements are the individual participants. In order to create chemical change, we have to be prepared to change personally and to interact significantly with others. This is what happens in real teamwork and the result is superior performance. Unfortunately, many teams are actually just groups that are unable to reach their potential. If you do not have both team leadership and group facilitation skills, put them at the top of your personal development list. In the meantime, ensure that you are demonstrating team behavior.

> *He who knows others is wise. He who knows himself is enlightened.*
>
> Tao Te Ching

Develop Influencing Skills

To be successful we must be able to influence others, often in situations which might be stressful: perhaps advocating to be the first in line for a promotion or hanging on to your job, getting the backer you definitely need to get your start up off the ground or getting buy-in to a decision that others see as less than advantageous to themselves.

The first step to influencing in these circumstances is to avoid being adversarial and to create a comfortable environment—even if we do not feel comfortable ourselves. Influencers are alert to the needs of those they wish to influence and try to address those needs by way of either the style or content of their proposal. People in sales are trained to change the emphasis of a presentation depending on the buyer. For example, in selling a new piece of equipment to senior management, the salesperson might focus on cost savings and how the equipment could give the company a competitive edge. In a presentation to frontline supervisors, focus might be on ease of use, productivity enhancements, and training and technical support. Everyone you influence has a need, whether it be a business need or a personal one.

Very often effective influencers automatically mirror the style and language of the other person. This makes it easy for the other to first understand and second buy the idea. Learning to understand your Personal Task/Process Style profile and that of others can help you develop that ability if it does not come naturally to you. If, for example, you have a strong preference for the Inward-Looking dimension and are highly detail-oriented, you are likely to communicate your ideas with considerable detail. If the individual you wish to influence is more Outward-Looking, they are likely to become impatient with details, and will quickly lose interest in what you are saying. Understanding another's style, and meeting the needs of that style, does not mean being calculating or manipulative. It is a matter of communicating so the other person can hear you.

Effective influencers not only instinctively tune in to people, but make a conscious effort to understand them. They care for others and have the ability to make the people around them feel good about themselves. In addition to this being a good value based thing to do, people who are positive and have high self-esteem are much more open to ideas and willing to support others than people who feel insecure or uncared for—an obvious principle that is too often overlooked.

It is easier to support someone who is filled with enthusiasm for, and belief in, what they are doing. Enthusiasm is catching and can carry people to "yes!"

The final common denominator of effective influencers is their ability to communicate that enthusiasm. Our success is measured by the contribution we make. But we seldom can make a contribution single-handedly. We need others to provide information or resources, or to share the load. Power used to come from the formal authority of a position. Today, most people's major source of power is their influencing ability. People who influence can get things done.

If you feel that you are lacking influence, check your product image and packaging against the guidelines described in this chapter, as well as the practices presented in the Workouts for Getting Interconnected.

WORKOUTS FOR PROMOTING YOURSELF

See Appendix A: How to Approach the Workouts.

1. Create Synergy: Be a Team Player

We're going to ask you to take a simulated astral flight. As you answer the next few questions, imagine an out-of-body experience in which you have a bird's-eye view of yourself at work or in a situation in which you are interacting with a group of people. This observation from afar can help you to increase your objectivity and think in terms of real-life examples rather than generalities. When answering theoretically, we are likely to respond as we would like or intend to behave, not as we actually do behave. The traits described in the questions below are those most often identified when team members voice concerns about members whom they see as not being team players.

Rate each on a 1-to-4 scale—1 being no, never or seldom, and 4 being definitely or all of the time.

1. Do you readily share information with others?	1 2 3 4
2. Do you seek information from others?	1 2 3 4
3. Are you receptive to constructive feedback?	1 2 3 4
4. Do you give others constructive feedback?	1 2 3 4
5. Do you have the skills to give and receive constructive feedback?	1 2 3 4
6. Do you participate fully in meetings/discussions?	1 2 3 4
7. Do you fully share the load?	1 2 3 4
8. Do you communicate effectively with others?	1 2 3 4
9. Do you take initiative?	1 2 3 4
10. Do you feel responsible for not only your contribution to the team, but the success of the team as a whole?	1 2 3 4
11. Do you readily help others develop by sharing your knowledge?	1 2 3 4
12. Do you have a positive attitude even when the situation may not appear to be positive to you?	1 2 3 4
13. Are you able to work effectively with others in spite of personal differences?	1 2 3 4
14. Do you ensure that concerns or issues are openly and quickly addressed?	1 2 3 4
15. Are you flexible in your opinions and open to new ways of doing things?	1 2 3 4
16. Once you've openly explored options, do you stand firm on positions you believe in?	1 2 3 4
17. Do you take time to get to know your teammates?	1 2 3 4

Rating: If you have a score of 60 to 68, you have a great deal to offer a team and should be able to demonstrate team skills that will differentiate you.

If your score is 48 to 60, you are able to contribute quite effectively in a team environment. With conscious effort directed toward the areas in which you rated lowest, you can raise your profile as a strong team member.

A score of less than 48 indicates that you are missing an opportunity to differentiate yourself and enhance your persona.

2. See Yourself as a Product

Note: Several of the following workouts ask you to think of yourself as a product. They are designed to help you gain clarity regarding what you have to offer, and to express it clearly, simply and impressively. With this knowledge, you will be able to identify opportunities more readily and respond to them quickly and effectively.

1. Think of any product. How would you describe it? Jot down the qualities that come to mind. These will include qualities of the product itself, and possibly the service that goes with it.
2. Now, think of yourself as a product. How would people describe you?
3. Ask the same question of someone you know who will answer honestly. Check their list against yours.

5. Spiff Up Your Packaging

1. Put yourself in a relaxed reflective mode.
2. Do a rerun in your mind of parts of your day. Visualize yourself as someone else would have seen you. Start with your arrival at work or at a client's office.

3. Check all details:
   - How did you look, from shoes to hair?
   - What was your demeanor: smiling, happy, serious, stressed?
   - If you greeted someone, what did you say? Were you warm and sincerely interested, distracted, abrupt?

     There are lots of stories about people being asked "How are you?" and answering "Not so well. I've got a serious problem with my gall bladder," and receiving the response "Glad to hear it." Even if you are not embarrassingly distracted or uninterested, the lack of interest always shows in your voice or eyes.

4. Skip through your entire day, dropping in at various points to check yourself out. How do you stand, sit, speak, shake hands, and make presentations? Would you be impressed if you were meeting yourself for the first time?
5. Note any opportunities for upgrading your packaging.

6. Be There

1. List what you do now that increases your visibility.
2. Think of other opportunities to raise your profile.
3. Put a plan into place to pursue these opportunities.

7. Believe in Yourself—Damn, I'm Good

Lack of confidence is a disease that spread in the nineties. Recession, downsizing and high unemployment all created situations that sapped many people's confidence. If yours is shattered, or even a little shaky, then following can help you tap the best of yourself during the day.

1. When you wake up in the morning, before you even get out of bed, repeat to yourself, "I'm (your name) and damn, I'm good!"

2. Say it over and over until you feel the energy and confidence surging through you. If you are alone, say it out loud, but it can be just as effective if you shout it silently in your mind.
3. If you feel your confidence slipping during the day, find a spot (even the subway will do), relax your body and mind, and repeat.

A Vignette

Destiny of Choice: The Power of Winner Instinct

Diane felt completely powerless.

For several years, she sought ways to control what seemed to be the uncontrollable. The world she suddenly found herself in was so foreign to her that she says she felt she had been abducted by aliens. One minute, she was an independent woman, successfully supporting her two daughters; the next, she was experiencing an unpredictable and frightening reality that meant counting pennies on her dresser top to buy food for her children and going days without food herself—and even facing homelessness.

It all began when Diane, who had worked in customer service for a manufacturing company, lost her job during a downsizing. Optimistic by nature and confident of her abilities, she had no doubt that she would find another job quickly. But few companies were hiring, and several weeks and a countless number of resumes later, Burnett's unemployment insurance ran out; she was stunned to find herself on welfare.

Despite her misery, she managed to learn and grow. She recognized that if she were ever to get back to a normal existence, she had to do things *differently*. She knew that the old rules of job hunting and success were no longer guiding the play. But what were the new rules? In her search for them she realized that her success depended on her changing herself. It depended on the number and quality of her connections, and her ability to get people's attention and to sell herself.

Although depression sometimes paralyzed her to the point where she couldn't get out of bed, she managed to make calls and slowly build a network. She laughingly says that she became the "network fanatic." She also recognized the importance of *disconnecting* from the wrong people, and moved away from negative acquaintances.

One day, Diane told herself that it was time to quit thinking about herself and start helping others. She called the United Way and offered to become a volunteer. She became an active, hard-working volunteer, doing whatever was required, from rising early and traveling across the city by public transit to set up fundraising events, to lugging heavy boxes. Every activity became an opportunity to contribute, to learn and to make contacts. Soon she was leading fundraising projects. She loved what she was doing, even though she wasn't earning money. Her volunteer work gave her a great deal of satisfaction.

However, she found it more and more difficult to pay her rent and began to slip behind. Just when she felt that she couldn't be more powerless, welfare cuts were instituted, making it impossible for her to meet her financial commitments.

Diane came home one day to find an eviction notice stuck on the door of the apartment that had been her family's home for ten years. She was terrified. How could her life have deteriorated to this point? Where could she take her children? Who could she turn to for help?

But she had learned well the importance of interconnectedness. She forced herself to pick up the phone and call a reporter who had written a series in the local newspaper on downsizing and its effect on people. Perhaps the reporter knew of someone who could help Burnett with her eviction case.

When the reporter heard Diane's story, she decided to write a piece on her for the newspaper. A local businessman read it and offered Burnett and her children a house to live in, providing she paid the heat and utilities. Ironically, her welfare income was cut further as a result. So despite the assistance she was not ahead financially.

Still, she described the move as "kismet." She believed that it was meant to be. The house was in the neighborhood where she'd grown up, and she intuitively knew that there was a reason she was being called back, that something good would happen. She felt at home in her neighborhood. Many people in the area had known her parents, and knew her. It was easier to make contacts and to get involved. Soon she was active in the community.

Only three years after she came close to experiencing homelessness for herself and her children, she had her own fundraising business and had become an active contributor to her community. The skills she developed; her determination, enthusiasm, proactivity, ability to sell herself in spite of lots of opportunity to lose her self-confidence; and the support of many people with whom she built relationships—all made it possible for her to create her own success.

Diane used *winner instinct* to succeed.

Throughout her bleak experience, Diane continued to learn. She read, thoughtfully and honestly examined herself, and took courses. She changed personally in many ways. She broke the procrastination habit. Although she had always gotten along well with people, she learned to be more flexible. She learned to say no. She learned how to access her intuition, which she sees as an essential resource in making decisions regarding business opportunities and people. But most importantly, she recognized that she "had to learn that things aren't others' fault. Whatever happens comes from within. Our experience comes from the choices we make."

When we have winner instinct, we develop an inner locus of control. We know that our personal success and happiness depend not on luck or arbitrary circumstances, but on our ability to respond effectively by being in tune with the laws of the new world. Does having winner instinct guarantee that nothing "bad" will ever happen to us? No, but it drastically reduces the likelihood. And it does guarantee that negative experience is a challenge to which we can effectively respond, and then we can move ahead to create our own unique success story.

Appendix A

HOW TO APPROACH THE WORKOUTS

Getting Started

Workouts often comprise several steps. To properly prepare yourself, completely read each workout before you start. Keep a Winner Instinct notebook with a Success Moments section, in which you can jot down examples of your successes, and instances in which you feel more in tune with the laws of success than you were in the past. Remember, reinforcing and celebrating what you do well is as important as recognizing what you could do better!

Ideally, devote half an hour per day, for four to five days per week, for six weeks. You will be able to focus on one law per week. Though you will not complete all workouts in this time, you will be able to tackle those that can help you to develop in areas that are important to you.

Find a quiet corner, away from interruptions. Have at hand your notebook and a pen, and remember to do the following:

- Capture Winner Instinct ideas
- Complete the workouts
- Develop your personal commitments to growth.

Getting Reflective

> We dance around in a ring and suppose, But the secret sits in the middle and knows.
>
> Robert Frost

Some workouts will ask you to put yourself into a relaxed reflective mode. This is to allow you to reflect more clearly and better tap your intuition. When instructed to do so, use the following steps:

1. Close your eyes.
2. Begin breathing slowly and deeply.
3. Consciously relax your muscles—particularly those that carry your tension (shoulders, jaw, neck).
4. If your mind is still racing, use one of the following visualization relaxation techniques:
   - As you inhale, picture the air you are inhaling and color it—whatever color is soothing to you. As you exhale, picture the air you are exhaling and color it—a color that represents feelings you want to release, perhaps red or black. Or
   - As you breathe deeply and slowly, picture a stream and beside it a large oak tree with brilliant fall foliage. Picture leaves, slowly dropping, one by one, from the branches, floating down and settling on the water.
5. Once you feel more relaxed (for some "perfectly" relaxed may take practice), move into the workout.

Picture It

Some of the workouts include a technique that has been found by many to accelerate personal growth: visualization.

At one time, visualization was left to the New Agers and Eastern mystics. "Oh, sure," the skeptics scoffed. "Just picture it and it will come true!" Athletes were the ones who brought the practice into the mainstream; they believed that visualization increased their performance. In a study, one team practiced as usual for several weeks, while another only visualized itself practicing during the same time. The team that actually practiced improved performance by 24 percent. The team that only visualized improved its performance by 23 percent. The researchers theorized that, with visualization, your mind records only perfect maneuvers, whereas in actual practice, you do make mistakes.

Visualization can take the following three forms:

- Seeing yourself doing whatever it is you want to do, and doing it the way you want to do it. In this case you are watching yourself.
- Visualizing the experience as you would see it. You would visualize what and who is around you, from a first-person perspective.
- Overlaying your response (feelings) to the experience on either of the above. The feeling may be joy, excitement, or whatever the individual believes she would actually feel during the experience and as she achieves success. This is the most powerful.

Appendix B

HOW TO DEVELOP THE ART OF CONFLICT

Warning: If you do not handle conflict well, or if you avoid conflict, developing the art of conflict means opening yourself to personal change.

As you read the following section, think of a conflict in which you have been involved and assess how skillfully (or not) you handled it.

Detach and Reframe

Attachment is the great fabrication of illusions; reality can be attained only by someone who is detached.

Simone Weil

Conflict is not inherently bad. It is how we respond to it that characterizes a situation. As soon as our response is "Alarm! Alarm!" or "Problem! Problem!" we limit our chances of success.

Successful people see conflict as simply another challenge that has potential rewards. It is part of "the game." This detached view means that the emotion that for many of us often envelops conflict situations and clouds the facts, limits our success and not infrequently causes us to embarrass ourselves, is not aroused.

Being detached gives one a clearer perspective on which issues are important to push—if only to ensure that people understand your perspective—and which ones can be safely ignored. It means responding with energy, but not reacting with anger. It allows us to separate the problem from the person we see as being the source of the problem. It means attacking the issue—often with energy—without destroying a relationship. It means being able to continue to see and appreciate your partner-in-conflict's strengths.

As soon as we choose to react with emotion rather than respond with logic, our partner-in-conflict has the advantage. And we do choose. People often try to deflect responsibility: "He makes me so mad!" or "She gives me stress." This is like trying to deflect a boomerang. You have to grab it and put it away. In this case, accept ownership for the emotion and embrace the personal growth required to manage it. It is easier for some people than for others to detach themselves from their own and others' emotions, but with practice, everyone can.

Acquire Understanding

1. *Of the Other Person*

An old saying says, "Know thine enemy." But your partner-in-conflict is more likely to be someone on the same side as you—although it may not feel like it. Whether it's a business partner, your investor, a teammate or a life partner, truly trying to know them is essential to your artful handling of conflict. We can never understand the thousands of life events that led the other person to a particular position or action, however close the relationship, but we can better understand them at this moment in time, and recognize their humanness—if we are generous enough to do so.

Although their behavior or ideas may conflict with ours, and they may not meet our expectations, most people are doing the best they can with what they have and where they are at this moment. Being artful in conflict is more difficult if we dislike our sparring partners. If we cannot find anything within a person to feel positive about, it is impossible to make a connection, and if there is no connection, there will be no solution. People who achieve what they set out to achieve in life have learned this.

> *If we could read the secret history of our enemies, we should find in each man's life sorrow and suffering enough to disarm all hostility.*
>
> Longfellow

2. *Of the Other Person's Position*

It may take work, it may take probing, it may mean fighting your own perceptions, but get yourself to the point where you understand your partner-in-conflict's position. You cannot participate artfully in a conflict if you do not understand the other's motivations or concerns.

Keep in mind that agreeing and understanding are very different. Afterward, you may still not agree with another's position, but you will be better equipped to address it.

3. *Of Yourself*

Be honest with yourself about your own behavior and motivation. Well-intentioned people are capable of unconsciously rewriting the history of their actions to fit a version with which they are comfortable, then slipping the altered version into their memory bank. If we force ourselves to self-examine, we can find the original under the rewritten version.

After an honest examination, ask yourself whether your position is still justified. If it is, stand firm. If not, admit the error of your position. Doing so is really not a "big deal": the other person knows you are wrong anyway!

> *Nothing is so easy as to deceive one's self; for what we wish, we readily believe.*
>
> Demosthenes

Rules for Resolution

Be Fair

Be fair in your negotiations to resolve conflict. Any ground greedily taken from your opponent will not support you well in the long run. If you have an ongoing relationship with the individual, his inevitable resentment will eventually motivate him to find a way to repay you. Even if you never work with that person again, remember the old saying "What goes around, comes around." Someday, somehow, you are likely to lose any advantage you gained.

Assess the Consequences

Think of a shark and its prey. Once its jaws are locked, it will not let go. People in conflict, spurred on by anger or pride, metaphorically often behave in the same way. No matter what the consequences, they won't let go. They are not even aware of the consequences. If you follow the earlier step of detachment, you should be able to weigh the consequences. How important to you is the position you are taking in the conflict? What might happen if you don't let go? Is it worth it?

John was the company's controller. He worked closely with the CEO and from the beginning had felt that that his boss didn't like him. No matter what John recommended, the CEO never granted his approval.

Their hottest point of conflict was John's careful perusal of the CEO's expense statements. The CEO consistently disagreed with John's request for a detailed expense account. John believed that what he was doing was right and refused to relent.

Within a few months John was fired. The consequences were high, but John knew the risk he was taking and held firm.

In the short term, the consequences were painful. In the longer term, John established his own business and found more joy in work than he ever had in the past. The CEO, who was constantly in conflict, died at a relatively young age of a sudden heart attack.

Become an Artful Dodger

It is the emotion that gets you. Negative conflict seldom results from issues—it results from the negative emotions triggered by the actions or differences. If you can avoid the emotional hook, you'll either prevent the negative conflict completely or free yourself to deal with it artfully.

Be Elegant

A little bit of class always holds you in good stead. Take the high road. Be gracious about the points on which you have to give. Don't waste energy and mar your image by bad-mouthing your conflict partner.

Be Creative

Creativity can open new paths to a solution. When people are "locked" in conflict, they are also often "locked" into their positions. Look for other routes that will allow you to reach your end, and that the other person can travel with comparative ease. Caution: This is not the same as compromise. You are not accepting less—you are looking for a different route by which to achieve the same personal outcome. Compromise is sometimes appropriate, but beware compromise that waters down the best outcomes so that everyone goes away half happy, and no one achieves what they want or more importantly need.

Be Firm

Once you have detached yourself emotionally, tried to understand, self-examined, checked your position for fairness, considered the consequences and decided you can handle them, stand coolly and sensitively firm.

Never Gloat

Win/win is a laudatory concept, but is often not possible from the point of view of the nature of the conflict. There can be win/win, however, if you ensure that you never jeopardize the pride or self-worth of your partner-in-conflict. A master of the art of conflict never gloats or demeans the other person.

Does mastering the art of conflict mean you will always win? No, but you will have the best possible shot at it and won't beat yourself up afterwards over what you should have done differently. You will definitely win in the longer term by developing the reputation of an individual who knows what he wants and goes for it, but does so with integrity and style. Every time you engage in conflict artfully, you enhance your reputation and build your power to influence.

Get to the Root of Conflict

The Roots of Conflict

Understanding the root of a conflict can give clues to the solution. The following are examples of what might be discovered, and how that insight might be used. It is not intended to be a pat prescription. Each conflict issue includes a myriad of variables that makes it unique and complex. This section is designed to give you a sense only of how you might apply the Roots of Conflict framework.

As you read the discussion of each root, ask yourself the following: Does this play a role in the conflict I am experiencing? If the answer is yes, consider trying the highlighted suggestions.

Values

Our organizations have, for the most part, become more diverse and open and this has led to more complexity. When people come from different cultures and backgrounds, they inevitably bring their own values with them. As corporate cultures become more open, people feel freer to bring personal values, which used to be left at the door, into the workplace—and to apply them. There is little one does that does not have a connection of some kind with values, but some issues are more value laden than others and can therefore be more sensitive and lead more easily to conflict.

Sometimes this is predictable. Other times it is a complete surprise. One organization that we provided consulting services to had instituted an employee-of-the-month program, assuming that everyone appreciated individual recognition and at least a few minutes of personal glory. Soon after the program was implemented, a star performer who had moved recently from the Far East was the recipient. To the surprise of the company, the moment of the announcement was not a happy one for her. The attention embarrassed her. "Please," she asked, "give the reward to my team."

This opened the reward system to discussion, and the company found that it was not only people with cultural differences who were uncomfortable with the concept of the award. Several people with North American roots did not like to be the center of attention. For them, the award was not a motivator. Many people value other kinds of rewards, such as a quiet thank-you or the offer of a challenging project. Others quite openly cite money as their motivator.

When conflict is rooted in differing values

- **Reflect individually**
  Identify the different values at play. Ask yourself whether the value you are holding that is contributing to the conflict is actually important to you, or whether you are reacting out of habit. Would you be able to accept the other person's value? If not, can you propose a middle ground that would work for both of you and would not compromise the outcome?
- **Reflect together**
  Acknowledge and discuss each value so that each participant better understands the other's viewpoint. Look for things you have in common. Look for a way to find a process or solution that is less heavily value based. Discuss whether either of you would be willing to accept the other's value. If not, search for a middle ground that will not jeopardize outcomes.

Agendas

Different agendas must first be acknowledged. If you suspect a hidden agenda, you must decide whether the conflict is sufficiently destructive to warrant discussing your perception with the other person.

> When there seems to be a hidden agenda
>
> First use the valuable feedback criteria described previously.
>
> - A hidden agenda is not a fact until it is acknowledged, no matter how sure you are that it exists. Think about what that person has done that gives you the impression that they have their own agenda.
> - Analyze the negative impact that the (perceived) hidden agenda has on your relationship and on the group, and on getting the job done.
> - If the agenda is not one the other is likely to relinquish, consider how the multiple agendas might co-exist.

Work Styles

Use the Personal Task/Process Style Indicator as a tool to give you a framework for your reflection and any subsequent discussion.

Consider your preferred dimensions, and those you believe to be the preference of the coworker with whom you are in conflict. The differences you identify may be the source of your conflict. For example, if that individual has a strong preference for the Divergent dimension, and you scored much higher in the Convergent, you could have a frustrating working relationship. You are ready for closure and have already moved ahead long before your coworker, who wants to continue to discuss things even when the answer is obvious to you. Your coworker wants to stop and examine the group process, when you are already behind schedule and just want to get the job done!

When work styles clash

- Acknowledge the differences

Sometimes simply acknowledging the differences that are creating conflict helps. For example, in one workshop where teammates were examining their Personal Task/Process profile and comparing notes, I overheard one fellow comment to another, "Now I know why you drive me crazy. You'll probably still drive me crazy, but I think I can handle it better now that I understand you a little more."

- Make an effort to accommodate your coworkers' needs

When a dimension is particularly high, it means that we are most comfortable working in that mode. If your co-worker hasn't talked through an issue sufficiently to fully buy in, but you are feeling pressured by deadlines and are picturing your coworker talking straight through to the next meeting, you might curtail things by acknowledging the individual's needs and suggesting a compromise that will allow *your* needs to be met as well. "I know you'd like to talk about this some more. I'm worried about the time pressures we're under. How about we agree to discuss this for another ten minutes at the outside, and then move along?"

Personalities

Personality differences are more than just work differences. Something about the individual's behavior or attitude annoys you, and possibly vice versa. Or you may simply not like one another. It is commonly said that you don't have to like someone to work with them. True, but sometimes that is easier said than done.

In one team development workshop that I led, there were two participants—Dave and Frank—who were in constant conflict. For one exercise, they were working in different groups. The exercise was designed to encourage groups to come up with very different solutions to a single problem. One group (Dave's) felt that another group (Frank's) had worked unfairly. In the debriefing, Dave concluded strongly, "I know exactly what happened. Frank talked the rest of the group into throwing the rest of us to the wolves."

When personality differences are the root of your conflict

- As objectively as possible, look for the other individual's strengths and skills or knowledge—assets that you could benefit from, but may be cutting yourself off from.
- List what bothers you about them. Then examine the list. How important is it in the scheme of things? Do they always have to have the last word, or do they always criticize others? These behaviors may not be pleasant, but unless they actually create negative outcomes, they perhaps aren't enough to worry about. *Is the real problem the individual's irritating behavior, or your reaction to it?*

- If you and another person have an obvious two-way conflict, such as always looking for fault with one another and disagreeing with one another, or perhaps even not speaking, try to identify the cause of the conflict. Did something precipitate it? If so, would resolving that incident heal the wound? I once worked with a group in which two people worked side by side and had not spoken in 12 years. What started the conflict, neither could remember. All they knew was that they were enemies. Perhaps your conflict, too, is more habit than substance.
- Consider whether addressing the difference with the other party would be productive. If the conflict is hindering your ability to work at your peak potential, then it may be important to do so. If you decide to, you might use Valuable Feedback Criteria.
- One of the simplest and often best ways of dealing with personality conflict is to look for opportunities to get to know the other person better. (I know it is the *last* thing you want to do.) I once overheard two good friends talking, and one asked the other, "Remember when we used to hate each other's guts?" Once we get to know one another, we can sometimes find our differences to be complementary.

His comments were complete conjecture, since he had no way of knowing what had happened in the other group, but to him that was irrelevant. He didn't have to be there, he thought, to know exactly what had transpired, because he believed he knew Frank inside out: Frank could not be trusted. I happened to be observing Frank's group, and the fact was that Frank had actually been the member who insisted that his team play fairly, although not everyone listened. Even though the facts showed that Frank was not only not a "bad guy," but that he had played the "good guy," his sparring partner was reluctant to give up his belief that "it was all Frank's fault."

Winner's Tip: When considering conflict that results from either different work styles or personalities, keep in mind that we often have more to learn from people who are different from us than we do from those who are like-minded.

Miscommunication

Of all the roots of conflict, miscommunication is the most common. The good news is that it's also the easiest to prevent. Miscommunication happens most often when we are in a hurry—which many people would say means all of the time—and when we make assumptions about the other person's understanding of what we have said or agreed to do, and vice versa. Miscommunication is often the result of insufficient or sloppy communication. Vigilance is the key.

When you need to repair communication

- Did someone not pass on information as they should have?
- Was communication clear?
- Were expectations of one another clear?
- Did you play a part in the miscommunication?
- What can be done now to resolve the conflict?
- What should you now communicate, and to whom?
- What can be done to prevent miscommunication the next time?

Prepare to share your thoughts with the appropriate person.

Appendix C

THE PERSONAL TASK/ PROCESS STYLE INDICATOR

The Personal Task/Process Style Indicator was first introduced in Leslie's book *Organization 2000.* As a result of the positive feedback received from people who found it helpful, I decided to "play it again" in *Winner Instinct.* This is a revised version.

1. Complete The Personal Task/Process Style Indicator below.
2. Examine your profile using the Dimension Descriptors.
3. Consider the following: Does your profile support or hinder your winner instinct—that is, does it support or hinder your connection with each of the 6 New Laws of Success? For example,

- the Interactive, Attached, Outward-Looking and Divergent dimensions all support being in tune with Law #4: Get Interconnected.
- the Outward-Looking, Intuitive and Divergent dimensions support Law #5: Tap Your Intuition.
- a reasonable balance in each dimension supports Law #3: Walk Fast on Thin Ice.

- the Interactive and Outward-Looking dimensions support Law #6: Promote Yourself.
- the Outward-Looking, Divergent and Attached dimensions support Law #2: Embrace the New Renaissance.

From this, you can see that having a strong process focus is essential to being in tune with the six laws. However, if your profile is tilted too far to the process side, you will see and grab all the opportunities but will not have the follow-through and closure ability to bring them to fruition.

Personal Task/Process Style Indicator

Each individual has his or her own task/process orientation. Answer the following questions to identify your own. There are no "right" answers. Base your response to the statements on how you prefer to work, or what comes most naturally to you. The higher the rating, the stronger your preference.

Rate both (a) and (b) statements: (a) and (b) must add up to 5 in any combination. Each rating must be a whole number.

e.g. (a) 2	(b) 3
(a) 1	(b) 4
(a) 5	(b) 0

1. (a) To re-energize, I prefer quiet time alone.
   Score ______

1. (b) To re-energize, I prefer to be active with other people.
   Score ______

2. (a) In meetings, my focus is on the information being discussed.
   Score ______

2. (b) In meetings, I am very aware of people's reactions and body language.
   Score ______

3. (a) I prefer to focus on theory.
Score ______

3. (b) I prefer to focus on task/application.
Score ______

4. (a) I prefer to be "doing."
Score ______

4. (b) I prefer to be "thinking."
Score ______

5. (a) I prefer to push for closure on issues.
Score ______

5. (b) I prefer to let closure happen when the group is ready.
Score ______

6. (a) I prefer to develop ideas by brainstorming with others.
Score ______

6. (b) I prefer to develop ideas by reflecting on my own.
Score ______

7. (a) I like to be recognized for my critical-thinking abilities.
Score ______

7. (b) I like to be recognized for my empathy.
Score ______

8. (a) I find developing goals and objectives satisfying.
Score ______

8. (b) I find working on missions, visions and values statements satisfying.
Score ______

9. (a) I prefer solving problems in a step-by-step fashion.
Score ______

9. (b) I prefer solving problems by brainstorming for solutions.
Score ______

10. (a) I prefer knowing what to expect.
Score ______

10. (b) I prefer dealing with the unexpected.
Score ______

11. (a) I prefer to solve problems by looking to others for their experience/input.
Score ______

11. (b) I prefer to solve problems by drawing on my own experience.
Score ______

12. (a) I am influenced by inspirational, motivated individuals who speak with emotion.

Score _____

12. (b) I am influenced by individuals who present a case rationally, supported by concrete examples or data.

Score _____

13. (a) When faced with a problem, my first instinct is to analyze the problem, the causes and the implications.

Score _____

13. (b) When faced with a problem, my first instinct is to generate solutions.

Score _____

14. (a) I prefer being recognized for my creativity.

Score _____

14. (b) I prefer being recognized for my logic.

Score _____

15. (a) I easily see others' points of view.

Score _____

15. (b) I have firm beliefs about right and wrong, or what will work and what won't.

Score _____

16. (a) In casual conversation, I enjoy sharing information about myself.

Score _____

16. (b) In casual conversation, I prefer the focus to be on the other person(s).

Score _____

17. (a) I work toward the best solution, even if it may not be supported by everyone.

Score _____

17. (b) I work toward the solution that can be best supported by the group.

Score _____

18. (a) I read broadly.

Score _____

18. (b) I read material pertaining to my own industry/area of expertise.

Score _____

19. (a) I prefer trying something new.

Score ______

19. (b) I prefer using methods that have worked for me before.

Score ______

20. (a) I prefer carefully gathering and considering all information before making decisions.

Score ______

20. (b) I prefer making decisions quickly based on information at hand.

Score ______

21. (a) It seldom occurs to me to share information about what I am doing unless asked.

Score ______

21. (b) I enjoy sharing information about what I am doing and look for opportunities to do so.

Score ______

22. (a) I make decisions based on my beliefs and feelings.

Score ______

22. (b) I make decisions based on facts and figures.

Score ______

23. (a) I prefer to focus on the detail.

Score ______

23. (b) I prefer to focus on the idea.

Score ______

24. (a) I prefer thinking about what could be.

Score ______

24. (b) I prefer dealing with what is.

Score ______

25. (a) I prefer working to plan.

Score ______

25. (b) I prefer working according to needs as they arise.

Score ______

26. (a) I enjoy talking with others about my experiences and successes.

Score ______

26. (b) In conversation, I prefer talking about other rather than myself.

Score ______

27. (a) I judge people on their intentions.

Score _____

27. (b) I judge people on the outcomes they produce.

Score _____

28. (a) I enjoy responsibilities that require attention to detail.

Score _____

28. (b) I find dealing with detail tedious.

Score _____

29. (a) My decisions are most strongly influenced by facts and figures.

Score _____

29. (b) My decisions are most strongly influenced by my sense of what is best.

Score _____

30. (a) I like to stick to a schedule.

Score _____

30. (b) I prefer to use schedules as general guidelines to be changed as needed.

Score _____

Scoring Sheet

Transfer your scores for each statement to the appropriate spaces below. Note: Record your scores carefully—(a)s and (b)s are at times reversed.

Independent	**Interactive**
1.(a)	1.(b)
6.(b)	6.(a)
11.(b)	11.(a)
16.(a)	16.(b)
21.(a)	21.(b)
26.(b)	26.(a)
Total _________	**Total** _______

Detached	Attached
12.(b)	12.(a)
17.(a)	17.(b)
22.(b)	22.(a)
27.(b)	27.(a)
Total ________	**Total** _______
Inward-Looking	**Outward-Looking**
3.(b)	3.(a)
8.(a)	8.(b)
13.(b)	13.(a)
18.(b)	18.(a)
23.(a)	23.(b)
28.(a)	28.(b)
Total ________	**Total** _______
Logical	**Intuitive**
4.(a)	4.(b)
9.(a)	9.(b)
14.(b)	14.(a)
19.(b)	19.(a)
24.(b)	24.(a)
29.(a)	29.(b)
Total ________	**Total** _______
Convergent	**Divergent**
5.(a)	5.(b)

10.(a)	10.(b)
15.(b)	15.(a)
20.(b)	20.(a)
25.(a)	25.(b)
30.(a)	30.(b)
Total ________	**Total** _______

Now transfer your totals to the Style Profile that follows.

Style Profile

Task-Focused		Process-Focused	
Independent	_______	Interactive	_______
Detached	_______	Attached	_______
Inward-Looking	_______	Outward-Looking	_______
Logical	_______	Intuitive	_______
Convergent	_______	Divergent	_______
Total	_______	**Total**	_______

Interpretation

Dimension Scores

If a score ranges from 14 to 16 for each dimension pair, the individual can probably work comfortably across the dimensions and move back and forth between the two as appropriate. A score of 17+ indicates a preferred dimension. A preferred dimension describes the way in which an individual works most comfortably and therefore most easily. It does not mean that certain individuals are unable to demonstrate that dimension's opposite; however, they probably have to remind themselves to do so. The greater the difference between the scores of the dimensions in a pair (e.g., Independent/Interactive), the greater the difficulty in demonstrating the behaviors associated with the weaker dimension.

Total Scores

A Task score of 80+ suggests a Task orientation.

A Process score of 80+ suggests a Process orientation.

A score of Task 70 to Process 80 or Task 80 to Process 70 suggests the individual is a synthesizer—one who moves comfortably and appropriately between Task focus and Process focus. It is easier for synthesizers to meet the expectations of the new world of work.

Note: A higher score under one dimension does not necessarily mean that all the characteristics of that dimension apply to you, nor that none of the opposite dimension apply to you. This would only be the case if you had a score of 30 to 0 for a pair of dimensions.

Dimension Descriptors

Independent/Interactive

Individuals who show a preference for the independent mode:

- Work best independently.
- Can be disadvantaged in group work—they often develop ideas best by thinking quietly on their own, and a group discussion can block rather than stimulate their thinking.

- Often do not think of communicating information with others, as they do not have a strong need to interact with others. Because they do not share information readily, they can be misunderstood and seen as hoarding information and being secretive or aloof.
- Do not necessarily want to retreat to a cabin in the woods but do look to solitary activities to re-energize.

Individuals who show a preference for the interactive mode:

- Need people around them and re-energize by being active with others. They work best with others.
- Need interaction to stimulate their thought processes. They thrive on meetings, think well out loud and may dominate discussion.
- Need variety.

Detached/Attached

Individuals with a preference for the detached mode:

- Are able to stand emotionally back from issues and examine them with detachment—they separate facts from emotion and use the facts; they recognize and test assumptions.
- Can miss people factors.
- Do not value opinions that are not proven by fact.
- Take pride in being sensible and level-headed.
- Others' opinions of them are not of great concern to them.

Individuals who have a preference for the attached mode:

- Become emotionally involved in issues. May show emotion.
- Are aware of and consider others' feelings.
- Are more strongly influenced by feelings than logic.
- Are moved by emotional pleas or motivational presentations.
- Create energy and enthusiasm for ideas they support.

Inward Looking/Outward Looking

Individuals who have a preference for the inward-looking mode:

- Focus most intently on their immediate environment including the job at hand.
- Work well with detail and see the detail easily and clearly—they can get caught up dotting i's and crossing t's and miss the bigger picture.
- Like to have clear goals and objectives.
- Like structure.
- Tend to focus on their particular area of expertise and not to develop broad interests or become a generalist.

Individuals with a preference for the outward-looking mode:

- Are tuned into the bigger picture.
- May overlook details.
- Speak in broad terms and generalities.
- Would prefer developing a mission statement or strategic plan to developing goals and objectives.
- Enjoy exploring the theory behind an application and cause and effects of issues.
- Value being well versed in many topics.

Logical/Intuitive

Individuals who have a preference for the logical mode:

- Need the world to make sense.
- Like to approach things in a logical step-by-step fashion.
- Believe things and issues should be easily resolved with a little common sense, and to them issues are straightforward.

- Prefer to work with structured models when problem solving. Wide-open brainstorming or "blue skying" has little appeal for them.
- Prefer a structured work environment.

Individuals with a preference for the intuitive mode:

- Like to think and explore possibilities.
- Are not limited by a need for structure or preconceived ideas.
- Are open to all possibilities.
- Like to try new approaches.
- Like to problem solve by freewheeling brainstorming.
- Generate creative ideas.
- Are not comfortable working in a highly structured environment or mode.
- Often examine issues from different, and not apparently logical, perspectives.

Convergent/Divergent

Individuals with a preference for the convergent mode:

- Have very firm opinions.
- Live comfortably with their decisions, feeling confident that they are right.
- Are quick to make decisions and change their mind very reluctantly.
- Become impatient with any discussion they see as wheel spinning.
- Like to work to plan.
- Often play the role of moving things to closure.
- Are likely to supply answers—to tell, rather than ask questions.

Individuals with a preference for the divergent mode:

- Like to gather as much information as possible.
- Are open to others' points of view.
- Carefully consider all information and opinions.
- Like a discussion to run its own course and to reach closure when the group is ready.
- Take a facilitative or coaching approach to dealing with people, asking rather than telling.
- Enjoy working with the unexpected and dealing with needs as they arise.
- Look for compromise.

Appendix D

STRENGTHENING SELF-CONFIDENCE

GROW YOUR SELF-CONFIDENCE

People who aren't by nature self-confident have to find a way of acquiring the attribute. Those who have developed it cite a number of requirements. If possessing confidence is a challenge for you, you might use the following self- development checklist.

- ❑ Have a dream and a clear personal definition of success.
- ❑ Be determined to fulfill the dream. Make a list of all the steps you can take right now to begin moving towards your dream.
- ❑ Force yourself to do things that are not always comfortable. Start by choosing one action that will take you closer to your goal, but that you have been putting off doing because it requires that you to step outside of your comfort zone. Take action and follow through on it.
- ❑ Face a fear and realize that 'there is nothing to fear, but fear itself'. Ask yourself, "What is the worst that can happen if I do this?" and, "How will I feel if I *don't* do this?"

- ❑ Realize that your past failures, missed-opportunities, and all of your 'shoulda, woulda, couldas' don't dictate your present or your future.
- ❑ Recognize and internalize that it is O.K. not to be perfect. If we were, we wouldn't be human.
- ❑ Treat perceived failures dispassionately as learning experiences. Identify the learnings you can take away and be sure to apply them. It is amazing how often we go on and on, as they say "doing the same thing and expecting different results."

❑ Be conscious of your self-talk. As Mahatma Ghandi said, "*A man is but the product of his thoughts - what he thinks, he becomes.* "

❑ Open a personal success account and make deposits regularly by recognizing and feeling good about even small successes.

❑ Draw on this account when you think you have "failed" or "blown it" (remember all of the times you have succeeded and draw on those feelings to propel you forward).

- ❑ Fake it until you make it. If you don't feel confident simply play the part of how you would think and behave if you were filled with confidence. Soon acting will become reality.

Without purpose and passion, we have neither clear direction nor the fuel to drive us. We spend more time struggling with the challenges than grabbing the opportunities. Success eludes us.

Appendix E

TIPS FOR APPLYING WINNER INSTINCT TO YOUR SITUATION

The 6 New Laws of Success apply to each of us. As you will have discovered, however, some apply more than others, depending on our personal makeup or current situation.

The following five tips each pertain to the laws in a specific circumstance. Check out the one that applies to you at this particular time.

1. Tips for Starting Out As An Entrepreneur

As an entrepreneur starting out, your big challenge is keeping your balance. Your probable preference for horizontal behaviors and activities makes you at home in a world of hyper-change. Your big-picture thinking and never-ending new ideas create marvelous energy and enormous possibility. Not infrequently, however, entrepreneurs do not realize these possibilities because they lack focus and attention to detail.

Check Your Focus

Focus as clearly as possible. You may be multitalented, but don't try to be everything to everyone. Decide what business you are in—what you do for whom—and stick to it. Don't be tempted to do other things for monetary reasons only. If you don't know what you are offering, how can your prospective customers be expected to know?

Get Organized

Put a structure in place—and stick to it. Ensure that on a daily basis, or at least weekly, you allot appropriate time for marketing, business management, new relationships or connecting, environmental scanning, following through on sundry ideas, and time for daydreaming, which is really opening the door to your intuition. Don't book every minute of your day—for most entrepreneurs this would be too structured to allow them to work comfortably and at their peak.

Pay Attention to Details

The details can get you. Putting enough details into proposals for clients, checking the fine print, communicating specifically, firming up agreements by putting them in writing, keeping track of receipts (how many do you have stuffed in a pocket right now?)—none of these are likely to be on your list of "fun stuff" if you are entrepreneurial. Force yourself to pay attention to important detail, and if you can't, hand off what you can to someone else. Hire people to take over the day-to-day administration as soon as you can afford to do so, and free yourself up to do what you do best.

Live With Purpose and Passion

Entrepreneurs, more than perhaps any others, have to be on purpose. When Howard Schultz, CEO of Starbucks, was asked what qualities it takes to be a successful entrepreneur, he answered, "You have to have a great tolerance for pain! You have to work hard, and have so much enthusiasm for one thing that most other things in your life have to be sacrificed."

Entrepreneurs are so driven by the idea and the excitement of possibilities that they don't mind the pain. They love every minute that they are engrossed in their venture. If you are feeling too much pain, perhaps you are not on purpose.

Be Contagious

If you are truly excited about your vision, others will catch your passion. If you are not excited, then you need to do some rethinking.

Promote Yourself

An entrepreneurial venture requires that you first sell yourself to potential partners, investors, bankers and customers. They must "buy you" in order to buy your unproven idea. If you are truly enthused about your product, and convey that enthusiasm, then you will sell yourself and your idea simultaneously.

Sell an Image

Some people go to great effort to create an impression. Faith Popcorn tells the story of starting up her business in a ground-floor professional suite. When a senior vice-president of a large company asked to tour their offices before he assigned them a project, she created what she called "the world's first virtual office." She rented the whole top floor of rooms in an impressive building and brought in desks, computers, drawing tables, phones connected to nowhere, and created a "staff" made up of freelancers and friends. They didn't get the assignment, but Popcorn found it a useful lesson. It emphasized for her that "if the vision is there, the means will follow."

Today, for the most part, small startups can have as much credibility as larger firms, as long as the principal players have a solid track record.

The "natural" salesperson has to be careful not to become overzealous, which can result in overselling. Zealous entrepreneurs not infrequently sell themselves as they envision themselves being in the future, rather than as they are now. It may be to your advantage to look bigger in some competitive situations, but it is an easy slide into misrepresenting what you do. You will eventually be unable to meet expectations and will lose credibility.

Image has more value than reality.

To last, image must be built only as truths.

Derek Lee Armstrong

The Persona Principle

Act on Your Intuition

How many good ideas that could move you forward have you not gotten around to acting on this week? For starters, there's the great marketing idea that you had in the middle of the night that you intended to put in a letter to clients, and the person you met at a dinner party last week whom you have a good "feeling" about but have not yet called. Your probable response is "I'm too busy." If so, then you are ignoring the edge that your intuition is offering you.

2. Tips for Heading a Growing Enterprise

You are on your way to the big time. Your entrepreneurial idea is proving itself to be every bit as successful as you knew it would be. Your operation is growing by leaps and bounds. You have to hustle to keep up with the increasing demand for your product or service. You may even have attracted investors or have proudly announced yourself on the stock exchange. Your dream is becoming a reality.

At this stage, entrepreneurs frequently experience a common ailment. Although everything should be great, it is getting tougher to get up in the morning. The joy in the heart has been replaced with a definite queasiness in the stomach.

You are experiencing growing pains. And this kind of growing pain can be fatal.

As a startup entrepreneurial company moves to the next level of growth, a new organizational personality evolves, and critical new needs emerge. The idyllic dreams of childhood are replaced by the realities of adulthood.

The following is a common scenario at this stage of growth.

> The founders and their closely knit group of startup employees lament that things are no longer the way they used to be—when they worked hard, played hard, and were driven by the dream. ("So what if we don't make anything this year? Let's bet on the dream.") Now, overhead, more employee mouths

to feed, and perhaps shareholders' and investors' expectations force a more pragmatic approach. You struggle to find a way to keep the cheer alive, while addressing your new world realities. Everyone used to be in harmony, and giving everything they had to the dream. Any little squabbles were out in the open, and were settled quickly over lunch. Everyone was easily involved in decisions, so everyone had the same information and was automatically onboard and pulling in the same direction.

Now you are not so sure. Some people are resisting your direction, and, you suspect, going their own way on a lot of things. Communication is breaking down. Information that is obvious to you doesn't seem to have gotten out clearly to the employees. You hear rumors of petty conflicts that you are convinced are impeding momentum. You don't want a lot of structure. You want to keep a spontaneous, easy-going environment, but it seems people are working a cross-purposes at times, and inventing their own procedures.

It is time to get a grip. You can grow while maintaining the dream, and the energy, and the cohesiveness that come with it—if you effectively apply the winner instinct principles.

Bring in a Manager

If you have not already brought in someone to oversee the day-to-day operations, now is the time. Not only are your greatest strengths unlikely to be management ones, you just don't have the time. You need to stay focused on the dream, the strategic direction, and whatever is required to move the company forward. But take great care in hiring someone. Don't let someone else take from you the decision about who should run the operation. Major investors have been known to interpret a young company's creative environment as chaos (and they may be right), and impose on it a "professional" manager. The result is often a horror story, conflict and wasted time (read dollars). *Don't give away your right to choose your own people!*

Remember, the "right" people are those that do the following:

- Get excited about your dream.
- Do not emphasize what's wrong with your organization and how they can fix it, but what's right with it and how they can help make it even better.
- Make you immediately comfortable and certain that you can develop an open relationship with them. (Don't let an impressive resume override your intuition. It is your intuition that has played a major role in getting you this far. Don't quit listening to it now!)
- Have had experience with small to mid-sized firms. Impressive experience in a large corporation will not guarantee that they can demonstrate the same success in your environment.

Don't Get Too Busy for People

You may be flying around the world, grabbing opportunities and making deals, building strategic alliances, building relationships with investors and perhaps a new board, negotiating with your bankers. You are almost never in the office, and besides, now you have managers to look after the internal stuff. Right? It is too easy to rationalize why you are not personally in touch with your people. No matter how long your To Do list, nor how important each item is, keeping in touch with people has to be permanently on the top—no matter what!

Live With Purpose and Passion

You are the holder of the company dream. That dream and your belief in it is what can give everyone who works in your company—whether shipper, receptionist or salesperson—a sense of purpose. That clear purpose will give them the energy and direction that will move the company ahead. Having others look after day-to-day operations allows you to focus strategically, and still have time to connect with people on your team.

The executive team cannot play Hercules and pull your company to the next level. There must be internal combustion that creates energy from within to drive the company.

You must be the major catalyst for that energy creation by keeping the dream in front of everyone, and letting them know that they play an essential part in fulfilling the dream—and that you appreciate them. When people know they are important to you, they make your priorities their priorities.

For this kind of energy, you need synergy. And synergy is created by team-based organizations.

Make Your Team Happen!

"But good teams just happen," you may be thinking. "We had one in the beginning. And we didn't do anything to make it happen." In your earlier life, you had a handful of people who were excited about the same idea and quite probably came together because they were compatible. Working hard and playing hard together, combined with the excitement over the project, melded you easily into a cohesive team.

As the company grows, however, teams have to be developed. A larger number of people with different values, priorities and working styles start appearing on the scene. We don't expect a sports team to just happen—why do we expect organizational teams to just happen?

You will not achieve the success you dream of and deserve if you do not have a team-based operation. An effective team base ensures the energy, cohesiveness, responsiveness and flexibility you need to get to the next level. The executive team must spark the energy, but a team is required to fan the flame, keep it burning, and efficiently use the energy produced.

Think about this—everyone knows teams create synergy when they are at play-2 + 2 = 5 or more. If you don't have teams, you have groups. In groups, 2 + 2 = 3 or less. So, if your company is made up of groups rather than effective teams, you are not only not reaping the benefits of teams—you are actually losing ground.

Get your whole team together to discuss and commit to actions to manage the issues that are emerging at your stage of growth. Ask questions like the following:

- How can we keep the dream alive as we grow?
- How can we get big, but still feel small?
- What are we doing that used to work but doesn't work as well anymore?

Keep the team process in front of everyone all the time. Teams will not happen if the team process is considered only once a year at an annual retreat. Managing the team process must become part of the task.

Make the Hard Decisions

If this applies to you, then you already know exactly to what and to whom in your organization I am referring. As you have grown, some people no longer fit. Perhaps their style and values do not suit a growing organization. More likely, they are not fully buying into the direction you know the company must now take. You've let things ride for lots of reasons: your long-standing relationship; their long-term relationship with important clients (an important consideration); or a particular skill they bring to the company. The reality is that their inability to fully buy in is at the very least slowing down your progress, and at the most undermining the company's success.

Employees and perhaps investors can also see what is happening, and the longer you wait to make the tough calls, the more likely it is that people's belief in your ability to lead will be eroded.

If you haven't had a firm heart-to-heart, clarifying your expectations and getting solid and evident commitment that those expectations will be met, start there. But expect changed behavior quickly. Not only are they no longer right for your organization, but your organization is no longer right for them. If they don't change quickly, do what needs to be done

Add Structure

Check communication systems, management systems, even meetings.

As you start moving to the next level, what was flexibility sometimes becomes limpness and chaos. Your growth will be impeded—perhaps even stopped if you don't have the appropriate structures in place. You do not want to go to the other extreme (i.e., rigid formality of procedures), but if you haven't done so already, it is time to formalize at least some of your organization's practices.

Get Rid of the Clutter

If yours is like most small companies, it grew from an organizational point of view, haphazardly. Seldom do small startup operations have the interest or the time for organization. Practices, informal policies and mind-sets sprout and grow. It is often the "little stuff" that seems to get in the way: an expense approval process that is too cumbersome, or an unwritten rule that issues wait for the bimonthly meeting to be addressed. Some of this small stuff may have served a purpose when first implemented. Now it is cluttering your company and getting in the way of serious growth.

At Mitel Corp., the things that get in the way are referred to as "sacred cows." Stephen Quesnelle, Mitel's head of quality, describes sacred cows as "the barriers that everybody knows about, but nobody talks about."33 Herds of sacred cows were a major part of the mismanaged growth that nearly felled Mitel in the early 1990s. Shares that were once traded for more than $33 were trading for less than $1. Killing sacred cows became part of the corporate culture, freeing Mitel to start growing again.

Mind Your Own Business

Big-dollar opportunities that you will be tempted to rationalize to yourself are bound to come along. "It is not quite what we are doing, but we could do it." It takes discipline to say no, particularly when you need to improve your cash flow. Resist! Not only will it dilute your focus and decrease the energy going to fulfill the dream, but it will blur your image. You have determined what you are best at—so be that.

3. Tips for Achieving Greater Success Within Your Organization

It is essential that you be in flow with all six laws. In addition to the workouts you selected, try the following:

1. **At the beginning of every workday, ask yourself these questions:**

    - What can I do today that will add value?
    - If I were working as an outside contractor, what would I do that would help to ensure that my contract would be renewed?

2. **At the end of every workday, ask yourself these questions:**

    - What did I accomplish today?
    - Did I use my time wisely?
    - Did I raise my profile?
    - What did I learn?
    - Whom did I help?
    - What did I do that makes my contribution particularly valuable?
    - Who knows about my unique contribution?

There is an expectation in successful organizations that everyone demonstrate leadership qualities.

4. Tips for Job Searching

The most important asset for a job searcher is belief in himself, but that is often the hardest to attain—and to maintain. Too many we'll-call-you's can make a dent in the strongest mettle. And many people are entering the job-search process with an already undermined self-esteem.

You may have lost your job in a restructuring exercise in an organization to which you have given your working life. You may have made errors in judgment that lost you your job and now make you question your ability. You may have entered the job market armed with a university degree for which you worked hard and felt proud, but which now, at times, seems insignificant in light of employers' high expectations. You may be feeling that you will never find another position at the same level, or with an equivalent title to the one you left.

Often loss of self-esteem is the result of the irrational conditioning that tells us that a title endorses our worth. A title has been the organizational equivalent of a knighthood, with all sorts of unspoken trappings attached. It has meant that you were recognized by those on high, and were therefore a little better than those without a title or with a lesser title. Being without a title, for many, erodes self-worth.

One particular high-tech firm, for example, reorganized around teams, and therefore managers became "team leaders." A manager confided to me that for over a year he told no one, not even his wife, that he was no longer a manager. Although he still played a key role in the organization and maintained his salary level, he lost his self-esteem along with his title.

A vice-president changed career paths and turned to teaching. In describing the change and the stress he was leaving behind, he said, "You know, I don't really have a position anymore, and I share a desk and have no admin support." Although stress-free, he felt somehow less than before.

If your self-esteem slips even occasionally, it is important to work on it. In addition to trying the workout, Believe in Yourself—Damn, I'm Good, try the following:

Part A

1. When your confidence slips, remind yourself of your strengths. Remember your successes. Remember how you felt when you succeeded. Recall positive comments you received. Remember you how felt when you received them.
2. Go into relaxed reflective mode. Imagine what feeling confident and successful feels like and looks like. Visualize yourself feeling "at home" wherever it is that you want to be.
3. Conjure up a feeling of success and total comfort with yourself.

Winner's Tip: *If visualization is difficult for you, look through magazines and find pictures that to you represent successful, confident people. Cut them out and create a collage. As often as you find beneficial, move into relaxed reflective mode and look at the collage, imagining what each confident person is feeling.*

Part B

1. If you feel your confidence is slipping when you are with others, do the following:
   - Stand or sit up taller.
   - Relax your muscles. Surreptitiously take a few breaths.
   - Put a sparkle in your eye. (With practice, you can do that—it is like smiling without using your mouth.)
   - Pretend! Recall the feeling of success and ease that you conjured in Part A. If we pretend often enough and combine the actions with feelings, eventually acting with confidence will begin to come to you naturally.
   - Get enthused.

Living With Purpose and Passion

Living with purpose and passion is very important for you. Apply for positions that excite you. (If the reality is that you need a job now, and nothing is immediately in view that excites you, find an aspect of another job that you can get enthused about.) Choose a company you would be excited and proud to work for. Once you have defined your purpose and found a job in which you can fulfill yourself, enthusiasm automatically follows.

We earlier described Dr. Phil Currie's deep belief that enthusiasm is critically important and how his feeling that "That's my job" landed a position for him.

Be Persistent

It is easier to be persistent if you are confident and enthused. Once you develop these characteristics, persistence will probably follow. However, if you have not fully mastered the first two, or are a procrastinator such that even enthusiasm cannot ignite you, then develop a system for yourself.

- Plan the next week—who you need to contact and how you will contact them.
- If making phone calls, plan what you will say.
- Break the plan down into days. Each morning, go over your commitments for the day and make yourself check each one off as you complete it.

Be In Touch and Keep Dreams Alive

Develop a directory of everyone you know. Get in touch. Let people know that you are job-searching. Tell them what you are looking for.

Ask for their help. Who do they know? Who might be able to help you? Develop the practice of contacting several people every day.

Know (don't just "hope"!) that eventually your tactics will work. Accept the present, however difficult it may seem, as is. Don't squander your energy on feeling bad about today. Focus positively on your dream for tomorrow.

5. Tips for Working Virtually

Spend Some Time at the Office

Find a productive reason to spend time at the office. Ideally, participate in a task force or committee.

That idea will not appeal if one of the reasons you chose to work at home was to avoid having to get involved in activities outside your immediate job. However, the phrase "out of sight, out of mind" applies readily to telecommuters. One of the benefits of working from home is that your performance is judged mainly on the quality and timeliness of your outputs. However, the downside is that you can easily be forgotten. You have to make an effort to be remembered.

Keep in Touch

Remember that the people you should be connecting with may be "out of sight, out of mind," too! Make a list of people you would benefit from keeping in touch with, as well as people you might help in some way. Include the following:

- People of influence within your company—partly to keep yourself in front of them, also to keep yourself informed about changes in the company.
- Co-workers who may or may not be telecommuters—to gain information not only about what is happening in the company, but also about what they are doing, the skills they are learning, the new information they are gaining.

Replenish Your Knowledge Base

When working on your own, it is easy to overlook the fact that your knowledge base is eroding. Subscribe to your industry journals and join an industry association. Keep plugged in via the Internet. Be cognizant that your knowledge ages. It is essential that you replenish it. Stop regularly to assess what you are doing, how you are doing it and whether you could be doing it better. Occasionally, ask the person you report to what you can do differently, or better. Don't wait for a formal evaluation.

About The Authors

Leslie Bendaly

Leslie is a best-selling author and an internationally respected leader in teamwork, leadership development and organizational change with over 30 years of experience. Leslie's models, tools and books are used in organizations worldwide to improve how people lead and work together. Leslie's books have been selected as mandatory reading for MBA and other postgraduate programs in both the United States and Canada and as handbooks for managers in companies such as IBM. She is founder and CEO of K&Co, a firm that has been helping teams and leaders to bring out the best in themselves for over 30 years.

Nicole Bendaly

Nicole is the president of K&Co. Her research in organizational behavior began almost 20 years ago and she now focuses her attention on helping organizations to develop the factors most critical to the performance of their teams and leaders. She has applied her research to the development and delivery of leadership and team development programs and assessment tools, a number of which are being used in over 200 organizations across North America. Nicole is a dynamic speaker and facilitator on topics impacting organizational, team and leadership performance, all of which help people to tap into the best of themselves and those they work with.

Services Available

K&Co is a leader in team and leadership performance and is best known for its Team Fitness Tool, a powerful team assessment and set of targeted tools to enable teams and leaders to maximize their performance.

K&Co offers workshops, consulting, keynote addresses, and customized team assessment and curriculum development.

The Team Fitness Tool

A web-based team development tool that includes a powerful team assessment and all the tools teams need to take action to leverage team strengths and address opportunities for improvement.

Learn more at: www.teamfitnesstool.com

Request a demo of the Team Fitness Tool: info@kand.co

Team Development

Experience our Power up your Team development process and gain:

- Improved communication, openness and trust among team members.
- Greater engagement and accountability for individual and team effectiveness.

- An understanding of what is required to perform consistently as a high functioning team
- New practices and behaviors that move the team to the next level of performance
- Motivated team members pulling together in the same direction
- The ability to reduce and manage conflict
- The tools needed to address team issues that derail the team's focus
- And much more.

Leadership Excellence Workshops

Highly interactive and customized sessions designed to ensure your leaders demonstrate the behaviors and practices most essential to your organization's results.

Keynote Addresses

K&Co speaker topics include:

- Developing a Winner Instinct
- Leadership on the Run
- Enabling Everyday Innovation
- When Getting Along Together Doesn't Equal Results
- What it Really Takes to Lead a High Performance Team
- How to Achieve Greater Results with Less Struggle
- Leading a Change Compatible Team

Learn More at www.kand.co

Request information at info@kand.co

Printed in the United States
By Bookmasters